CROCH

Flower Garden Pineapple Doilies™

General Information

Many of the products used in this pattern book can be purchased from local craft, fabric and variety stores or from the Annie's Attic Needlecraft Catalog *(see page 23 for catalog information).*

Roses & Pineapples

Design by Maggie Petsch

SKILL LEVEL
■■■□ INTERMEDIATE

FINISHED SIZE
16½ inches in diameter

MATERIALS
- ❏ J. & P. Coats Knit-Cro-Sheen size 10 crochet cotton:
  1 (150-yd) ball #15 shaded pink
  1 (325-yd) ball #1 white
- ❏ South Maid size 10 crochet cotton (350 yds per ball):
  1 ball #484 myrtle green
- ❏ Size 7/1.65mm steel crochet hook or size needed to obtain gauge
- ❏ Tapestry needle

GAUGE
Center rose = 2 inches in diameter

SPECIAL STITCHES
Cluster (cl): Holding back on hook last lp of each st, 2 dc in indicated ch sp, yo, pull through all lps on hook.

Annie's Attic, Berne, IN 46711 • AnniesAttic.com • *Flower Garden Pineapple Doilies* 1

Beginning cluster (beg cl): [Ch 2, dc] in ch sp indicated.
Cluster shell (cl shell): [Cl, ch 3, cl] in ch sp indicated.
Beginning cluster shell (beg cl shell): [Beg cl, ch 3, cl] in indicated st or sp.
Picot: Ch 4, sl st in fourth ch from hook.
Treble cluster (tr cl): Holding back on hook last lp of each st, 3 tr in indicated st or sp, yo, pull through all 4 lps on hook.
Treble decrease (tr dec): Yo 5 times, insert hook in fifth ch of next ch-11, yo, pull up a lp, [yo, pull through 2 lps on hook] 5 times *(2 lps rem on hook)*, yo 5 times, sk next 6 chs on next ch-11, insert hook in next ch, yo, pull up a lp, [yo, pull through 2 lps on hook] 5 times, yo, pull through 3 rem lps on hook.

INSTRUCTIONS
DOILY CENTER
Rose
Rnd 1: With shaded pink, ch 5, sl st in first ch to form a ring, ch 5 *(counts as first dc, ch-2)*, (dc, ch 2) 5 times in ring, join with sl st in third ch of beg ch-5. *(6 ch-2 sps)*
Rnd 2: (Sc, 3 dc, sc) in each ch-2 sp around, **do not join.** *(6 petals)*
Rnd 3: Working behind petals of last rnd, sc in joining st of rnd 1, ch 3, [sc in next sk dc of rnd 1, ch 3] around, join with sl st in beg sc.
Rnd 4: (Sc, 5 dc, sc) in each ch-3 sp around, **do not join.**
Rnd 5: Working behind petals of last rnd, sc in joining st of rnd 3, ch 4, [sc in next sk sc of rnd 3, ch 4] around, join with sl st in beg sc.
Rnd 6: (Sc, 3 dc, tr, 3 dc, sc) in each ch-4 sp around, **do not join.**
Rnd 7: Working behind petals of last rnd, sc in joining st of rnd 5, ch 5, [sc in next sk sc of rnd 5, ch 5] around, join.
Rnd 8: (Sc, 3 dc, 2 tr, 3 dc, sc) in each ch-5 sp around, **do not join.**
Rnd 9: Working behind petals of last rnd, sc in joining st of rnd 7, ch 6, [sc in next sk sc of rnd 7, ch 6] around, join.
Rnd 10: (Sc, 3 dc, 4 tr, 3 dc, sc) in each ch-6 sp around, **do not join.**
Rnd 11: Working behind petals of last rnd, sc in joining st of rnd 9, ch 7, [sc in next sk sc of rnd 7, ch 7] around, join. Fasten off.

Leaves
Row 1: With myrtle green, ch 7, sc in second ch from hook and in each of next 4 chs, 3 sc in last ch, working on opposite side of ch, sc in each of next 4 chs, turn.
Row 2: Ch 1, sk first sc, working in **back lps** *(see Stitch Guide)* only, sc in each of next 4 sc, 3 sc in next sc, sc in each of next 5 sc, turn.
Row 3: Ch 1, sk first sc, working in back lps only, sc in each of next 5 sc, 3 sc in next sc, sc in each of next 4 sc, turn.
Rows 4 & 5: Rep rows 2 and 3.
Row 6: Ch 1, sk first sc, working in back lps only, sc in each of next 4 sc, 2 sc in next sc, sl st in fourth ch of any unworked ch-7 on rnd 11 of Center Rose, sc in same st on Leaf as last sc, sc in each of next 5 sc. Fasten off.
Make five more leaves, joining each on row 6 to an unworked ch-7 sp on rnd 11 of Center Rose.

BRUGES LACE BAND
Row 1 (WS): With white, ch 9, dc in sixth ch from hook and in each of next 3 chs, turn. *(4 dc)*
Row 2: Ch 2, sl st in tip of any Leaf on Center Rose, ch 2, dc in each of next 4 dc, turn.
Rows 3–11: Ch 5, dc in each of next 4 dc, turn.
Row 12: Ch 2, sl st in tip of next Leaf on Center Rose, ch 2, dc in each of next 4 dc, turn.
Rows 13–60: Rep rows 3–12 consecutively, ending with row 10. At end of last row, leaving long end, fasten off.
With tapestry needle, sew tops of 4 dc of last row to foundation chs beneath 4 dc of row 1.

PINEAPPLE SECTION
Rnd 1: With RS facing, join white with sl st in any ch-5 sp on outer edge of Bruges Lace Band, ch 1, sc in same sp, [ch 6, sc in next ch-5 sp] around, ending with ch 2, tr in beg sc to form last ch-6 sp. *(30 ch-6 sps)*
Rnd 2: Beg cl shell *(see Special Stitches)* in ch sp just formed, ch 3, [**cl shell** *(see Special Stitches)* in next ch-6 sp, ch 3] around, join with sl st in top of beg cl. *(30 cl shells)*
Rnd 3: Sl st in first cl shell ch sp, beg cl shell in same ch sp, *ch 3, sc in next ch-3 sp, ch 3, cl shell in next cl shell, ch 3, sk next ch-3 sp**, cl shell in next cl shell, rep from * around, ending last rep at **, join.
Rnd 4: Sl st in first cl shell ch sp, beg cl shell in same ch sp, *ch 7, cl shell in next cl shell, ch 3**, cl shell in next cl shell, rep from * around, ending last rep at **, join.
Rnd 5: Sl st in first cl shell ch sp, beg cl shell in same ch sp, *ch 2, sk first ch of ch-7, tr in next ch, ch 5, sk 3 chs, tr in next ch, ch 2, cl shell in next cl shell, ch 3, sk next ch-3 sp**, cl shell in next cl shell, rep from * around, ending last rep at **, join.
Rnd 6: Sl st in first cl shell ch sp, beg cl shell in same ch sp, *ch 4, (dc, ch 3, dc) in third ch of ch-5 sp, ch 4, cl shell in next cl shell, ch 3, sk next ch-3 sp**, cl shell in next cl shell, rep from * around, ending last rep at **, join.
Rnd 7: Sl st in first cl shell ch sp, beg cl shell in same ch sp, *ch 4, sk next ch-4 sp, 7 tr in next ch-3 sp, ch 4, cl shell in next cl shell, ch 3**, cl shell in next cl shell, rep from * around, ending last rep at **, join.
Rnd 8: Sl st in first cl shell ch sp, beg cl shell in same ch sp, *ch 4, dc in next tr, [ch 1, dc in next tr] 6 times, ch 4, cl shell in next cl shell, ch 3**, cl shell in next cl shell, rep from * around, ending last rep at **, join.
Rnd 9: Sl st in first cl shell ch sp, beg cl shell in same ch sp, *ch 4, sc in next ch-1 sp, [ch 3, sc in next ch-1 sp] 5 times, ch 4, cl

shell in next cl shell, ch 3, sl st in next ch-3 sp, ch 3**, cl shell in next cl shell, rep from * around, ending last rep at **, join. **Do not fasten off.**

First Pineapple
Row 1 (RS): Sl st in first cl shell ch sp, beg cl shell in same ch sp, ch 4, sc in next ch-3 sp, [ch 3, sc in next ch-3 sp] 4 times, ch 4, cl shell in next cl shell leaving rem sts unworked, turn.

Row 2: Sl st in first cl shell ch sp, beg cl shell in same ch sp, ch 4, sc in next ch-3 sp, [ch 3, sc in next ch-3 sp] 3 times, ch 4, cl shell in next cl shell, turn.

Row 3: Sl st in first cl shell ch sp, beg cl shell in same ch sp, ch 4, sc in next ch-3 sp, [ch 3, sc in next ch-3 sp] twice, ch 4, cl shell in next cl shell, turn.

Row 4: Sl st in first cl shell ch sp, beg cl shell in same ch sp, ch 4, sc in next ch-3 sp, ch 3, sc in next ch-3 sp, ch 4, cl shell in next cl shell, turn.

Row 5: Sl st in first cl shell ch sp, beg cl shell in same sp, ch 4, sc in next ch-3 sp, ch 4, cl shell in next cl shell, turn.

Row 6: Sl st in first cl shell ch sp, beg cl shell in same ch sp, cl in next cl shell, ch 1, turn, sl st in ch-3 sp of beg cl shell, ch 1, turn, cl in same cl shell as last cl. Fasten off.

Remaining 14 Pineapples
Row 1: With RS facing, join white with sl st in next unworked cl shell ch sp on rnd 9 of Pineapple Section, rep row 1 of First Pineapple.

Rows 2–6: Rep rows 2–6 of First Pineapple.

ROSE BORDER
Roses
Rnds 1–5: Rep rnds 1–5 of Center Rose.

Rnd 6: [(Sc, 3 dc, tr, 3 dc, sc) in next ch-4 sp] 3 times, (sc, 3 dc, tr) in next ch-4 sp, sl st over end st of row 3 at right-hand side of any pineapple on Pineapple Section, (3 dc, sc) in same ch-4 sp on rose as last tr, (sc, 3 dc, tr, 3 dc, sc) in next ch-4 sp, (sc, 3 dc, tr) in next ch-4 sp, sl st over end st of row 3 at left side of next pineapple on Pineapple Section, (3 dc, sc) in same ch-4 sp on rose as last tr, **do not join.**

Row 7: Working behind petals of last rnd, sc in joining st of rnd 5, [ch 5, sc in next sk sc of rnd 5] 3 times. Fasten off.

Make 14 more roses, joining each as for first rose of Rose Border between rem pineapple points around.

LEAVES
Rows 1–3: Rep rows 1–3 of leaf for Center Rose.

Row 4: Sk first sc, working in back lps only, sc in each of next 4 sc, 2 sc in next sc, sl st in third ch of any ch-5 on row 7 of any rose of Rose Border, sc in same sc on leaf as last 2 sc, sc in each of next 5 sc on leaf. Fasten off.

Make and join two more leaves as for first leaf in two rem ch-5 sps on row 7 of same rose.

Make and join three leaves on each rem rose of Rose Border around.

EDGING
Rnd 1: Join white with sl st at tip of first Leaf to the right on any 3-Leaf group, *[ch 11, sl st in tip of next Leaf] twice, ch 11, sl st in sl st between 2 cl shells on last row of next pineapple, ch 11**, sl st in tip of first Leaf on next 3-Leaf group, rep from * around, ending last rep at **, join with sl st in tip of Leaf at base of beg ch-11.

Rnd 2: *Ch 1, sk next 2 chs, [dc, ch 1] 5 times in next ch, sk next 2 chs, sl st in next ch, ch 3, sk next 5 chs, [**tr cl** (see Special Stitches), **picot** (see Special Stitches), ch 1] 3 times in next sl st, tr cl in same sl st, ch 3, sk next 5 chs of next ch-11, sl st in next ch, ch 1, sk next 2 chs, (dc, ch 1) 5 times in next ch, sk next 2 chs, sl st in next sl st, ch 7, **tr dec** (see Special Stitches), (ch 5, sl st, ch 7, sl st, ch 5, sl st) in top of tr dec, ch 7, sk next 4 chs, sl st in next sl st, rep from * around. Fasten off.❑❑

Victorian Centerpiece

Design by Dot Drake

SKILL LEVEL
 INTERMEDIATE

FINISHED SIZE
18 inches across

MATERIALS
- J. & P. Coats Knit-Cro-Sheen size 10 crochet cotton:
  600 yds #42 cream
  150 yds #35 almond pink
- Size 7/1.65mm steel crochet hook or size needed to obtain gauge

GAUGE
Rnds 1–9 of Center Flower = 3½ inches across

SPECIAL STITCHES
Picot: Ch 3, sl st in third ch from hook.
Beginning shell (beg shell): (Ch 3—*counts as first dc*, dc, ch 2, 2 dc) in specified ch sp.
Shell: (2 dc, ch 2, 2 dc) in specified ch sp.
Treble cluster (tr cl): Holding back last lp of each st on hook, work 1 tr in each of next 3 sts, yo, and pull through all lps on hook.

INSTRUCTIONS
FLOWERS
Center Flower
Rnd 1: With almond pink, ch 12, sl st in first ch to form ring, ch 1, 24 sc in ring, join with sl st in beg sc. Fasten off. *(24 sc)*

Rnd 2: Join cream with sl st in any st, ch 6 *(counts as first dc and ch 3)*, sk next 2 sc, [dc in next st, ch 3, sk next 2 sc] around, join with sl st in third ch of beg ch-6. *(8 ch sps)*

Rnd 3: Sl st in first ch-3 sp, for **petals,** (sc, hdc, 3 dc, hdc, sc) in each ch-3 sp around, **do not join**. *(8 petals)*

Rnd 4: [Ch 6, working behind petals, sc in next dc of rnd 2] around, ch 6, join with sl st in base of beg ch-6.

Rnd 5: For **petals**, (sc, hdc, 7 dc, hdc, sc) in each ch sp around, **do not join.**

Rnd 6: [Ch 7, working behind petals, sc in next sc of rnd 4] around, ch 7, join with sl st in base of beg ch-7.

Rnd 7: For **petals,** (sc, hdc, dc, 9 tr, dc, hdc, sc) in each ch sp around, **do not join.**

Rnd 8: [Ch 8, working behind petals, sc in next sc on rnd 6] around, join with sl st in base of beg ch-8.

Rnd 9: (Sc, ch 2, dc, 5 tr, **picot**—*see Special Stitches*, 5 tr, dc, ch 2, sc) in each ch sp around, join with sl st in beg sc. Fasten off.

First Border Flower
Rnd 1: With almond pink, ch 12, sl st in first ch to form ring, ch 1, 24 sc in ring, join with sl st in beg sc. *(24 sc)*

Rnd 2: Ch 3, holding back last lp of each st on hook, tr in next sc, 2 tr in next sc, yo, pull through all lps on hook *(beg cl made)*, [ch 6, holding back last lp of each st on hook, tr in each of next 2 sc, 2 tr in next sc, yo, pull through all lps on hook *(cl made)*] around, ch 6, join with sl st in top of beg cluster. Fasten off. *(8 cls)*

Rnd 3: Join cream with sl st in any ch sp, (ch 1, 5 sc, ch 1, sc in picot on Center Flower, ch 1, sl st in top of last sc made, 5 sc) in same sp, (5 sc, picot, 5 sc) in each ch sp around, join. Fasten off.

Second–Seventh Border Flowers
Rnd 1: With almond pink, ch 12, sl st in first ch to form ring, ch 1, 24 sc in ring, join with sl st in beg sc. *(24 sc)*

Rnd 2: Ch 3, holding back last lp of each st on hook, tr in next sc, 2 tr in next sc, yo, pull through all lps on hook *(beg cl made)*, [ch 6, holding back last lp of each st on hook, tr in each of next 2 sc,

4 Flower Garden Pineapple Doilies • Annie's Attic, Berne, IN 46711 • AnniesAttic.com

2 tr in next sc, yo, pull through all lps on hook *(cl made)]* around, ch 6, join with sl st in top of beg cl. Fasten off. *(8 cls)*

Rnd 3: Work same as for rnd 3 of First Border Flower around to last 2 picots, then work joining as follows: [ch 1, sc in picot of previous flower, ch 1], work same as for rnd 3 to next picot, rep between [ ], complete rnd, join. Fasten off.

Eighth Border Flower
Rnd 1: With almond pink, ch 12, sl st in first ch to form ring, ch 1, 24 sc in ring, join with sl st in beg sc. *(24 sc)*
Rnd 2: Ch 3, holding back last lp of each st on hook, tr in next sc, 2 tr in next sc, yo, pull through all lps on hook *(beg cl made)*, [ch 6, holding back last lp of each st on hook, tr in each of next 2 sc, 2 tr in next sc, yo, pull through all lps on hook *(cl made)]* around, ch 6, join with sl st in top of beg cl. Fasten off. *(8 cls)*
Rnd 3: Work same as for rnd 3 of Second Border Flower, joining first 2 picots to First Border Flower and last 2 picots to Seventh Border Flower.

Border
Rnd 1: With RS facing, join cream with sl st in last free picot at left on any Border Flower, ch 1, sc in same picot, *ch 11, [sc in next picot, ch 7] twice**, sc in next picot, rep from * around, ending last rep at **, join with sl st in beg sc.
Rnd 2: [15 sc in next ch-11 sp, 10 sc in each of next 2 ch-7 sps] around, join.
Rnd 3: Ch 3 *(counts as first dc)*, dc in same st, *ch 2, 2 dc in next sc, ch 4, sk next 5 sc, (dc, ch 5, dc) in next sc, ch 4, sk next 5 sc, 2 dc in next sc, ch 2, 2 dc in next sc, ch 6, dc in sp between next 2 groups of 10 sc, ch 6**, 2 dc in first sc of next group of 15 sc, rep from * around, ending last rep at **, join with sl st in top of beg ch-3.
Rnd 4: Sl st to first ch-2 sp, **beg shell** *(see Special Stitches)* in same ch sp, *ch 3, 9 dc in next ch-5 sp, ch 3, **shell** *(see Special Stitches)* in next ch-2 sp, ch 5, sk next ch sp, 2 dc in next dc, ch 5**, shell in next ch-2 sp, rep from * around, ending last rep at **, join.
Rnd 5: Sl st to first ch-2 sp, beg shell in same ch sp, *ch 2, sk next ch sp, dc in next dc, [ch 1, dc in next dc] 8 times, ch 2, shell in next shell, ch 4, sk next ch sp, 2 dc in each of next 2 dc, ch 4**, shell in next shell, rep from * around, ending last rep at **, join.
Rnd 6: Sl st to first ch-2 sp, beg shell in same ch sp, *ch 4, sc in next ch-1 sp, [ch 3, sc in next ch-1 sp] 7 times, ch 4, shell in next shell, ch 4, sk next ch sp, dc in next dc, [ch 1, dc in next dc] 3 times, ch 4**, shell in next shell, rep from * around, ending last rep at **, join.
Rnd 7: Sl st to first ch-2 sp, beg shell in same sp, *ch 4, sc in next ch-3 sp, [ch 3, sc in next ch-3 sp] 6 times, ch 4, shell in next shell, ch 4, sk next ch sp, dc in next dc, ch 1, [(dc, ch 1, dc) in next dc, ch 1] twice, dc in next dc, ch 4**, shell in next shell, rep from * around, ending last rep at **, join.
Rnd 8: Sl st to first ch-2 sp, beg shell in same ch sp, *ch 4, sc in next ch-3 sp, [ch 3, sc in next ch-3 sp] 5 times, ch 4, shell in next shell, ch 4, sk next ch sp, dc in next dc, [ch 1, dc in next dc] 4 times, ch 1, (dc, ch 1, dc) in next dc, ch 4**, shell in next shell, rep from * around, ending last rep at **, join.
Rnd 9: Sl st to first ch-2 sp, beg shell in same ch sp, *ch 4, sc in next ch-3 sp, [ch 3, sc in next ch-3 sp] 4 times, ch 4, shell in next shell, ch 4, sk next ch sp, dc in next dc, [ch 1, dc in next dc] 6 times, ch 4**, shell in next shell, rep from * around, ending last rep at **, join.
Rnd 10: Sl st to first ch-2 sp, beg shell in same sp, *ch 4, sc in next ch-3 sp, [ch 3, sc in next ch-3 sp] 3 times, ch 4, shell in next shell, ch 4, sk next ch sp, dc in next dc, [ch 2, dc in next dc] 6 times, ch 4**, shell in next shell, rep from * around, ending last rep at **, join.
Rnd 11: Sl st to first ch-2 sp, beg shell in same ch sp, *ch 4, sc in next ch-3 sp, [ch 3, sc in next ch-3 sp] twice, ch 4, shell in next shell, ch 4, sk next ch sp, dc in next dc, [ch 1, dc in next dc] 6 times, ch 4**, shell in next shell, rep from * around, ending last rep at **, join.
Rnd 12: Sl st to first ch-2 sp, beg shell in same ch sp, *ch 4, sc in next ch-3 sp, ch 3, sc in next ch-3 sp, ch 4, shell in next shell, ch 5, sk next ch sp, sc in next dc, [(2 sc, picot, sc) in next ch-3 sp, sc in next dc] 6 times, ch 5**, shell in next shell, rep from * around, ending last rep at **, join.
Rnd 13: Sl st to first ch-2 sp, beg shell in same ch sp, *ch 4, sc in next ch-3 sp, ch 4, shell in next shell, ch 5, dc in next sc, [ch 4, sk next 3 sc and next picot, dc in next sc] 6 times, ch 5**, shell in next shell, rep from * around, ending last rep at **, join.
Rnd 14: Sl st to first ch-2 sp, beg shell in same ch sp, *ch 2, shell in next shell, ch 7, 6 sc in each of next 6 ch-4 sps, ch 7**, shell in next shell, rep from * around, ending with last rep at **, join.
Rnd 15: Sl st to first ch-2 sp, beg shell in same ch sp, *ch 2, 2 dc in next shell, ch 9, **tr cl** *(see Special Stitches)* over next 3 sc, [ch 5, tr cl] 11 times, ch 9**, 2 dc in next shell, rep from * around, ending last rep at **, join.
Rnd 16: Sl st to first ch-2 sp, ch 3, 2 dc in same ch sp, *[ch 5, sc in next ch sp] 13 times, ch 5**, 3 dc in next ch-2 sp, rep from * around, ending last rep at **, join. Fasten off.
Rnd 17: Join almond pink with sl st in center dc of any 3-dc group, ch 1, sc in same st, *(3 sc, ch 3, sl st in last sc made, ch 5, sl st in same sc, ch 3, sl st in same sc, 3 sc) in each of next 14 ch-5 sps**, sc in center dc of next 3-dc group, rep from * around, ending last rep at ** join. Fasten off.❏❏

Pineapple Basket

Design by Maggie Petsch

SKILL LEVEL
■■■■ EXPERIENCED

FINISHED SIZE
9 x 13 inches

MATERIALS
- J. & P. Coats Cotton Knit-Cro-Sheen size 10 crochet cotton (225 yds per ball): 1 ball white *(A)* Small amounts each shaded pinks *(B)*, mid rose *(C)*, shaded jades *(D)*, jade *(E)*, shaded light yellows *(F)* and canary yellow *(G)*
- Size 7/1.65mm steel crochet hook or size needed to obtain gauge
- Sewing needle
- Sewing thread

GAUGE
10 dc in row 1, and rows 1–4 = 1 inch
Basic daisy = 1½ inches in diameter

SPECIAL STITCHES
Shell: (3 dc, ch 2, 3 dc) in indicated st or ch sp of shell.
V stitch (V-st): (Dc, ch 3, dc) in indicated ch sp.
Double shell (dbl shell): (3 dc, ch 2, 2 dc, ch 2, 3 dc) in indicated st or ch sp.
Triple treble (trtr): Yo 4 times, insert hook in indicated ch sp, yo, pull up lp, [yo, pull through 2 lps on hook] 5 times.
3-triple treble cluster (3-trtr cl): Holding back on hook last lp of each st, work 3 trtr in indicated st or ch sp, yo, pull through all 4 lps on hook.

INSTRUCTIONS
BASKET
Row 1: Beg at bottom with A, ch 29, dc in fourth ch from hook and in each rem ch across, turn. *(27 dc, counting last 3 chs of foundation ch as first dc)*

Rnd 2: Ch 1, sc in each dc across, (sc, hdc, dc, hdc, sc) over side of turning ch-3, sc in rem lp of each ch across foundation ch, (sc, hdc, dc, hdc, sc) over side of last dc of row 1, join with sl st in beg sc, **do not turn.**

Row 3 (RS): Sl st in each of next 3 sc, ch 4, **shell** *(see Special Stitches)* in same st as last sl st, [sk next 4 sts, shell in next st] 4 times, tr in same st as last shell, leave rem sts unworked, turn.

Rows 4 & 5: Ch 4, shell in each of next 5 shells, tr in next ch-4 sp, turn.

Rows 6 & 7: Ch 4, shell in next shell, [ch 1, shell in next shell] 4 times, tr in next ch-4 sp, turn.

Row 8: Ch 4, shell in next shell, [ch 2, shell in next shell] 4 times, tr in next ch-4 sp, turn.

Row 9: Ch 4, shell in next shell, [ch 4, **V-st** *(see Special Stitches)* in next shell, ch 4, shell in next shell] twice, tr in next ch-4 sp, turn.

Row 10: Ch 4, shell in next shell, [ch 2, 8 dc in next V-st sp, ch 2, shell in next shell] twice, tr in next ch-4 sp, turn.

Row 11: Ch 4, shell in next shell, [ch 2, sk next ch-2 sp, dc in next dc, {ch 1, dc in next dc} 7 times, ch 2, shell in next shell] twice, tr in next ch-4 sp, turn.

Row 12: Ch 4, shell in next shell, [ch 4, sc in next ch-1 sp, {ch 3, sc in next ch-1 sp} 6 times, ch 4, shell in next shell] twice, tr in next ch-4 sp, turn.

Row 13: Ch 4, **dbl shell** *(see Special Stitches)* in next shell, [ch 4, sc in next ch-3 sp, {ch 3, sc in next ch-3 sp} 5 times, ch 4, dbl shell in next shell] twice, tr in next ch-4 sp, turn.

Row 14: Ch 4, shell in next ch-2 sp, ch 1, shell in next ch-2 sp, [ch 4, sc in next ch-3 sp, {ch 3, sc in next ch-3 sp} 4 times, ch 4, shell in next ch-2 sp, ch 1, shell in next ch-2 sp] twice, tr in next ch-4 sp, turn.

Row 15: Ch 4, shell in next shell, *ch 1, V-st in next ch-1 sp, ch 1, shell in next shell**, ch 4, sc in next ch-3 sp, [ch 3, sc in next ch-3 sp] 3 times, ch 4, shell in next shell, rep from * across, ending last rep at **, tr in next ch-4 sp, turn.

Row 16: Ch 4, shell in next shell, *ch 2, 9 dc in ch sp of next V-st, ch 2, shell in next shell**, ch 4, sc in next ch-3 sp, [ch 3, sc in next ch-3 sp] twice, ch 4, shell in next shell, rep from * across, ending last rep at **, tr in next ch-4 sp, turn.

Row 17: Ch 4, shell in next shell *ch 2, sk next ch-2 sp, dc in next dc, [ch 1, dc in next dc] 8 times, ch 2, shell in next shell**, ch 4, sc in next ch-3 sp, ch 3, sc in next ch-3 sp, ch 4, shell in next shell, rep from * across, ending last rep at **, tr in next ch-4 sp, turn.

Row 18: Ch 4, shell in next shell, *ch 4, sc in next ch-1 sp, [ch 3, sc in next ch-1 sp] 7 times, ch 4, shell in next shell**, ch 4, sc in next ch-3 sp, ch 4, shell in next shell, rep from * across, ending last rep at **, tr in next ch-4 sp, turn.

Row 19: Ch 4, shell in next shell, *ch 4, sc in next ch-3 sp, [ch 3, sc in next ch-3 sp] 6 times, ch 4**, shell in each of next 2 shells twice, rep from * across, ending last rep at **, shell in next shell, tr in next ch-4 sp, turn.

First Pineapple
Row 20: Ch 4, shell in next shell, ch 4, sc in next ch-3 sp, [ch 3, sc in next ch-3 sp] 5 times, ch 4, shell in next shell, tr between next 2 shells, turn.

Row 21: Ch 4, shell in next shell, ch 4, sc in next ch-3 sp, [ch 3, sc in next ch-3 sp] 4 times, ch 4, shell in next shell, tr in next ch-4 sp, turn.

Row 22: Ch 4, shell in next shell, ch 4, sc in next ch-3 sp, [ch 3, sc in next ch-3 sp] 3 times, ch 4, shell in next shell, tr in next ch-4 sp, turn.

Row 23: Ch 4, shell in next shell, ch 4, sc in next ch-3 sp, [ch 3, sc in next ch-3 sp] twice, ch 4, shell in next shell, tr in next ch-4 sp, turn.

Row 24: Ch 4, shell in next shell, ch 4, sc in next ch-3 sp, ch 3, sc in next ch-3 sp, ch 4, shell in next shell, tr in next ch-4 sp, turn.

Row 25: Ch 4, shell in next shell, ch 4, sc in next ch-3 sp, ch 4, shell in next shell, tr in next ch-4 sp, turn.

Row 26: Ch 4, shell in next shell sp, (3 dc, ch 1) in next shell sp, sl st in ch sp of last shell made, ch 1, 3 dc in same ch sp as last 3 dc made, tr in next ch-4 sp. Fasten off.

Center Pineapple
Row 20: With WS facing, join A with sl st in same sp between 2 shells on row 19 as last tr of row 20 of previous pineapple, rep row 20 of First Pineapple.

Rows 21–26: Rep rows 21–26 of First Pineapple.

Last Pineapple
Row 20: Rep row 20 of Center Pineapple, ending with tr in next ch-4 sp, turn.

Rows 21–26: Rep rows 21–26 of First Pineapple.

HANDLE
First Half
Row 1: With RS facing, join A with a sl st in end sp at outer edge of row 26 of end pineapple on right-hand side of basket, ch 4, shell between 2 shells of row 26, tr in next end sp of row 26, turn.

Rows 2–8: Ch 4, shell in next shell, tr in next ch-4 sp, turn.

Row 9: Ch 4, shell in next shell, dc in next ch-4 sp, turn.

Row 10: Ch 3, shell in next shell, tr in next ch-4 sp, turn.

Row 11: Ch 4, shell in next shell, dc in next ch-3 sp, turn.

Row 12: Rep row 10.

Row 13: Ch 4, shell in next shell, hdc in next ch-3 sp, turn.

Row 14: Ch 2, shell in next shell, tr in next ch-4 sp, turn.

Row 15: Ch 4, shell in next shell, hdc in next ch-2 sp, turn.

Row 16: Rep row 14.

Row 17: Ch 4, shell in next shell, dc in next ch-2 sp, turn.

Rows 18–26: Rep rows 10 and 11 alternately, at end of row 26, fasten off.

Second Half
Row 1: With WS facing, rep row 1 of first half.

Rows 2–25: Rep rows 2–25 of First Half.

Row 26: Ch 3, dc in ch-3 sp on row 26 of first half, (3 dc, ch 1) in next shell on row 25 of second half, sl st in shell on row 26 of first half, ch 1, 3 dc in same shell on row 26 of second half as last 3 dc, tr in next ch-4 sp on second half, ch 4, sl st in next end sp on row 26 of first half. Fasten off.

FLOWERS
Note: Working from instructions for Basic Daisy and Basic Starflower, and from chart for color and placement of Flowers, beg with Basic Daisy indicated on chart and work 23 Flowers, joining on rnd 2 to other Flowers and to Basket as indicated in instructions and on chart. Petals that overlap Basket and Handle and are not joined will be tacked down after all Flowers are completed.

Basic Daisy
Rnd 1: With color indicated on chart for daisy being worked, ch 6, sl st in first ch to form a ring, ch 5 *(counts as first dc, ch-2)*, (dc, ch 2) 5 times in ring, join with sl st in third ch of beg ch-5. Fasten off. *(6 ch-2 sps)*

Rnd 2: Join next color with sl st in any ch-2 sp, *(ch 5, **tr cl**—see Special Stitches, ch 5, sl st) in same ch sp, sl st in next ch sp, rep from * around, ending with sl st in same ch sp as beg ch-5. Fasten off. *(6 petals)*

To **join petals** of basic daisy on rnd 2 to tips of petals on other Flowers or over end sts of rows on Pineapple Basket, work petal to be joined until tr cl has been completed, remove hook from lp, insert hook in st or sp indicated on chart, pick up dropped lp, draw through st on hook, complete petal according to instructions for Basic Daisy.

Basic Starflower
Rnd 1: With color indicated on chart for starflower being worked, ch 4, 11 dc in fourth ch from hook, join with sl st in fourth ch of beg ch-4. Fasten off. *(12 dc, counting last 3 chs of beg ch-4 as first dc)*

Rnd 2: Join next color with sl st in any dc, [ch 6, sc in second ch from hook, dc in each of next 4 chs, sk next st, sl st in next st] around, ending with sl st in same st as beg ch-6. Fasten off. *(6 petals)*

To **join petals** of starflowers on rnd 2 to tips of petals of other flowers or over end sts of rows on Pineapple Basket, work petal to be joined until ch-6 has been completed, remove hook from lp, insert hook in st or sp indicated on chart, pick up dropped lp, draw through st on hook, complete petal according to instructions for basic starflower.

FINISHING
With sewing needle and thread, tack tips of Flowers that overlap Basket and Handle to Basket and Handle.❏❏

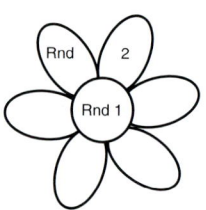
Basic Daisy

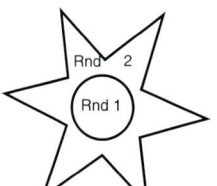
Basic Sunflower

COLOR KEY
A White
B Shaded pinks
C Mid rose
D Shaded jades
E Jade
F Shaded light yellows
G Canary yellow

STITCH KEY
○ Join petals

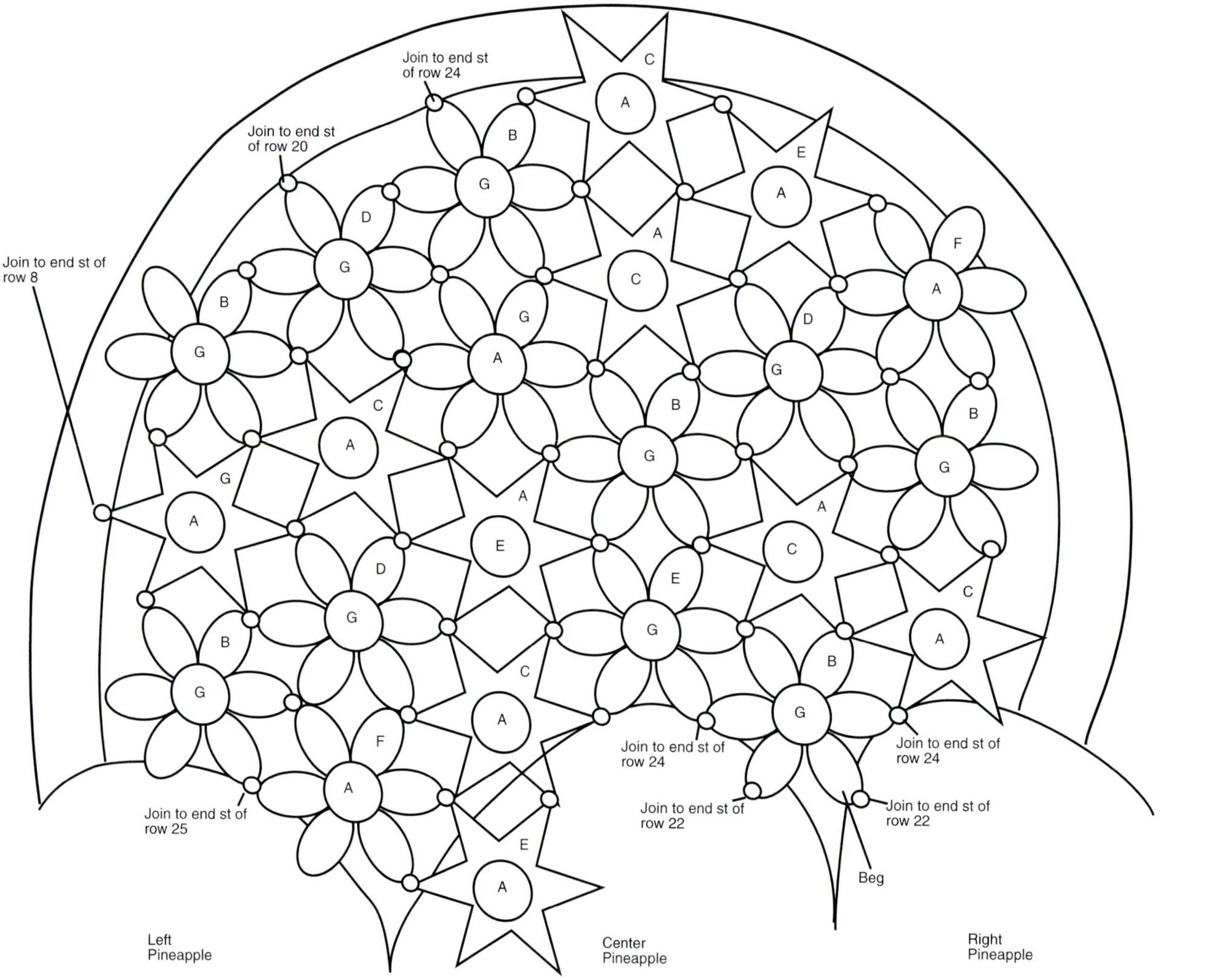

Left Pineapple

Center Pineapple

Right Pineapple

8 Flower Garden Pineapple Doilies • Annie's Attic, Berne, IN 46711 • AnniesAttic.com

Six Swans-a-Swimming

Design by Maggie Petsch

SKILL LEVEL
■■■□ INTERMEDIATE

FINISHED SIZE
14½ inches in diameter

MATERIALS
- South Maid size 10 crochet cotton (300 yds per ball):
    1 ball #13 shaded blues
- J. & P. Coats Knit-Cro-Sheen size 10 crochet cotton (225 yds per ball):
    1 ball #1 white
- 6-strand embroidery floss: Small amount gold
- Size 8/1.50mm steel crochet hook
- Size 7/1.65mm steel crochet hook or size needed to obtain gauge
- Tapestry needle
- Sewing needle
- Black sewing thread
- Seed beads:
    6 (⅛-inch) black

GAUGE
Lotus Flower = 2⅜ inches in diameter

SPECIAL STITCHES
Shell: (2 dc, ch 2, 2 dc) in ch sp.
Beginning shell (beg shell): (Ch 3—*counts as first dc*, dc, ch 2, 2 dc) in specified ch sp.
Double shell (dbl shell): (Shell, ch 2, 2 dc) in ch sp.
Beginning double shell (beg dbl shell): (Beg shell, ch 2, 2 dc) in ch sp.
Cluster (cl): Holding back on hook last lp of each st, 2 dc in indicated ch sp, yo, pull through all lps on hook.

INSTRUCTIONS
LOTUS FLOWER
Rnd 1: With size 7 hook and white, ch 3, 12 hdc in third ch from hook, join with sl st in beg hdc. *(12 hdc)*
Rnd 2: Ch 2 *(does not count as first st)*, 2 hdc in each hdc around, join, turn. Fasten off. *(24 hdc)*

First Inner Petal
Row 1 (RS): With size 7 hook, join white with sl st in single horizontal strand directly below **front lp** *(see Stitch Guide)* of any hdc, ch 3 *(counts as first dc throughout)*, working in single horizontal strand directly below front lp of each hdc, [2 dc in each of next 2 sts] twice, dc in next st, turn. *(6 dc)*
Row 2: Ch 3, dc in each of next 5 sts, turn. *(6 dc)*
Row 3: Ch 3, holding back on hook last lp of each st, dc in each of next 5 sts, yo, pull through all lps on hook, ch 1 to secure. Fasten off.

Remaining Five Inner Petals
Rows 1–3: With RS facing and size 7 hook, join white with sl st in horizontal strand directly below front lp of next unworked hdc on rnd 2, rep rows 1–3 of First Inner Petal.

First Outer Petal
Row 1: With RS facing and size 7 hook, working behind Inner Petals, sk first 2 sts of rnd 2 from the right edge of any Inner Petal, join white with sl st in front lp only of next hdc, ch 4 *(counts as first tr)*, working in front lps only, 2 tr in each of next 2 sts, tr in next st, turn. *(6 tr)*
Row 2: Ch 4, tr in each of next 5 sts, turn.
Row 3: Ch 4, holding back on hook last lp of each st, tr in each of next 5 sts, yo, pull through all lps on hook, ch 1 to secure. Fasten off.

Remaining Five Outer Petals
Rows 1–3: With RS facing and size 7 hook, join white with sl st in next unworked front lp on rnd 2, rep rows 1–3 of First Outer Petal.

DOILY

Rnd 1: With WS facing and size 7 hook, join shaded blues with sl st in **back lps** (see Stitch Guide) only of any hdc on rnd 2 of Lotus Flower, ch 7 (counts as first tr, ch-3), working in back lps only this rnd, [sk next st, tr in next st, ch 3] around, ending with sk last st, join with sl st in fourth ch of beg ch-7, turn. (12 ch-3 sps)

Rnd 2 (RS): Sl st in first ch-3 sp, **beg shell** (see Special Stitches) in same ch sp, *ch 2, dc in next ch sp, ch 2**, **shell** (see Special Stitches) in next ch sp, rep from * around, ending last rep at **, join with sl st in third ch of beg ch-3, **do not turn** at end of this or rem rnds. (6 shells)

Rnd 3: Sl st across to first ch sp of shell, beg shell in same ch sp, *ch 2, [dc in next ch-2 sp, ch 2] twice**, shell in ch sp of next shell, rep from * around, ending last rep at **, join.

Rnd 4: Sl st across to first ch sp, beg shell in shell, *ch 2, dc in next ch sp, ch 5, sk next ch sp, dc in next ch sp, ch 2**, shell in next shell, rep from * around, ending last rep at **, join.

Rnd 5: Sl st across to first ch sp, beg shell in same ch sp, *ch 3, sk next ch-2 sp, dc in next dc, ch 4, sk next 2 chs, sc in next sp, ch 4, dc in next dc, ch 2**, shell in next shell, rep from * around, ending last rep at **, join.

Rnd 6: Sl st across to first ch sp, beg shell in same ch sp, *ch 4, sk next ch-3 sp, dc in next dc, ch 4, **dc dec** (see Stitch Guide) in next 2 ch-4 sps, ch 4, dc in next dc, ch 4**, shell in next shell, rep from * around, ending last rep at **, join.

Rnd 7: Sl st across to first ch sp, beg shell in same ch sp, *ch 4, sk next ch-4 sp, dc in next dc, ch 11, sk next dc dec, dc in next dc, ch 4**, shell in next shell, rep from * around, ending last rep at **, join.

Rnd 8: Sl st across to first ch sp, beg shell in same ch sp, *ch 5, sk next ch-4 sp, dc in next dc, ch 4, sk next 2 chs, sc in next ch, ch 4, sk next 2 chs, dc in next ch, ch 4, sk next 2 chs, sc in next ch, ch 4, dc in next dc, ch 5**, shell in next shell, rep from * around, ending last rep at **, join.

Rnd 9: Sl st in each of first 2 dc and in shell, beg shell in same sp, *ch 3, sk next 2 chs, dc in next ch, ch 3, dc in next dc, [ch 4, dc dec in next 2 ch sps, ch 4, dc in next dc] twice, ch 3, sk next 2 chs, dc in next ch, ch 3**, shell in next shell, rep from * around, ending last rep at **, join.

Rnd 10: Sl st across to first ch sp, beg shell in same ch sp, *ch 3, sk next ch-3 sp, dc in next dc, [ch 11, sk next 3 ch sps, dc in next dc] twice, ch 3**, shell in next shell, rep from * around, ending last rep at **, join.

Rnd 11: Sl st across to first ch sp, **beg dbl shell** (see Special Stitches) in same ch sp, *ch 2, sk next ch-3 sp, dc in next dc [ch 4, sk next 2 chs, sc in next ch, ch 4, sk next 2 chs, dc in next ch, ch 4, sk next 2 chs, sc in next ch, ch 4, dc in next dc] twice, ch 2**, dbl shell in next shell, rep from * around, ending last rep at **, join.

Rnd 12: Sl st across to ch-2 sp, beg shell in same ch sp, *ch 2, shell in next ch-2 sp, sk next ch-2 sp, dc in next dc, [ch 4, dc dec in next 2 ch sps, ch 4, dc in next dc] 4 times, sk next ch-2 sp**, shell in next ch-2 sp, rep from * around, ending last rep at **, join.

Rnd 13: Sl st across to first ch sp, beg shell in same ch sp, *ch 2, dc in next ch-2 sp, ch 2, shell in next shell, ch 5, dc in top of next dc dec, ch 11, sk next 3 sps, dc in next dc, ch 11, sk next 3 sps, dc in next dc dec, ch 5**, shell in next shell, rep from * around, ending last rep at **, join.

Rnd 14: Sl st across to first ch sp, beg shell in same ch sp, *ch 2, sk next ch-2 sp, (dc, ch 4, dc) in next dc, ch 2, shell in next shell, sk next 2 chs, dc in next ch, ch 3, dc in next dc, [ch 4, sk next 2 chs, sc in next ch, ch 4, sk next 2 chs, sc in next ch, ch 4, dc in next dc] twice, ch 3, sk next 2 chs, dc in next ch**, shell in next shell, rep from * around, ending last rep at **, join.

Rnd 15: Sl st across to first ch sp, beg shell in same ch sp, *ch 2, 9 tr in next ch-4 sp, ch 2, shell in next shell, 2 sc in next ch-3 sp, 2 sc in next dc, [{2 sc in next sp} twice, 2 sc in next dc] 4 times, 2 sc in next ch sp**, shell in next shell, rep from * around, ending last rep at **, join.

First Pineapple

Row 1 (RS): Sl st across to first ch sp, beg shell in same ch sp, ch 2, tr in next tr, [ch 1, tr in next tr] 8 times, ch 2, shell in next shell, turn.

Row 2: Sl st across to first pineapple, beg shell in same ch sp, ch 3, [sc in next tr, ch 3] 9 times, shell in next shell, turn.

Row 3: Sl st across to first ch sp beg shell in same ch sp, ch 3, sk next ch-3 sp, [sc in next ch-3 sp, ch 3] 8 times, shell in next shell, turn.

Row 4: Sl st across to first ch sp, beg shell in same ch sp, ch 3, sk next ch-3 sp, [sc in next ch-3 sp, ch 3] 7 times, shell in next shell, turn.

Row 5: Sl st across to first ch sp, beg shell in same ch sp, ch 3, sk next ch-3 sp, [sc in next ch-3 sp, ch 3] 6 times, shell in next shell, turn.

Row 6: Sl st across to first ch sp, beg shell in same ch sp, ch 3, sk next ch-3 sp, [sc in next ch-3 sp, ch 3] 5 times, shell in next shell, turn.

Row 7: Sl st across to first ch sp, beg shell in same ch sp, ch 3, sk next ch-3 sp, [sc in next ch-3 sp, ch 3] 4 times, shell in next shell, turn.

Row 8: Sl st across to first ch sp, beg shell in same ch sp, ch 3, sk next ch-3 sp, [sc in next ch-3 sp, ch 3] 3 times, shell in next shell, turn.

Row 9: Sl st across to first ch sp, beg shell in same ch sp, ch 3, sk next ch-3 sp, [sc in next ch-3 sp, ch 3] twice, shell in next shell, turn.

Row 10: Sl st across to first ch sp, beg shell in same ch sp, ch 3, sk next ch-3 sp, sc in next ch-3 sp, ch 3, shell in next shell, turn.

Row 11: Sl st across to first ch sp, beg shell in same ch sp, 2 dc in next shell sp, ch 1, turn, sl st in last shell made, ch 1, turn, 2 dc in same shell as last 2 dc. Fasten off.

Remaining Five Pineapples
Row 1: With RS facing and size 7 hook, join shaded blues with sl st in next unworked shell on rnd 15, beg shell in same sp, ch 2, tr in next tr, [ch 1, tr in next tr] 8 times, ch 2, shell in next shell, turn.

Rows 2–11: Rep rows 2–11 of First Pineapple.

SWAN
Make 6.
Body
Row 1: With white and size 7 hook, ch 19, sc in second ch from hook and in each of next 16 chs, 3 sc in last ch, working on opposite side of ch, sc in each of next 16 chs, leave last ch unworked, turn.

Row 2: Working in back lps only, ch 1, sk first sc, sc in each of next 16 sc, 3 sc in next sc, sc in each of next 17 sc, leave last sc unworked, turn.

Row 3: Working in back lps only, ch 1, sk first sc, sc in each of next 17 sc, 3 sc in next sc, sc in each of next 16 sc, leave last sc unworked, turn.

Rows 4–9: Rep rows 2 and 3 alternately. At end of last row, fasten off.

Place marker in last st for bottom left corner of Swan.

Neck & Head
With WS facing and white and size 7 hook, ch 22, sc in second ch from hook, **hdc dec** *(see Stitch Guide)* in next 2 chs, hdc in each of next 10 chs, 2 hdc in each of next 7 chs, 7 hdc in last ch *(for head)*, sl st in rem lp of next st on opposite side of foundation ch. Fasten off.

Using photo as a guide, sew first 5 sts at bottom of neck to center sts of row 9 at right front of Swan with tapestry needle and white.

Feathers
With RS facing and Head of Swan toward you, with size 7 hook, join white with sl st in first rem lp on row 1 of Body, working in rem lps, [ch 4, sk next st, sl st in next st] across. Fasten off.

Join white with sl st in first rem lp on row 5 of Body, rep feathers for row 1.

Beak
With size 8 hook and 2 strands of gold embroidery floss, ch 3, sc in second ch from hook, dc in next ch. Leaving long end for sewing, fasten off.

With dc at right top edge, sew Beak to bottom of Head.

Eye
With sewing needle and black thread, sew one bead to center of Head.

Center Swan on rnd 15 of Doily between two pineapples. With tapestry needle and white, beg at marked st at bottom back of Swan, sew row 9 of Swan to rnd 15 of Doily approximately 1¼ inches across. Tack tip of tail to end st of row 4 on pineapple behind Swan. Tack bottom front of Neck to end st of row 2 on pineapple in front of Swan.

SMALL FLOWER
Make 6.

With white, ch 5, sl st in first ch to form ring, (ch 2, **cl**—*see Special Stitches*, ch 2, sl st) 6 times in ring. Fasten off.

With tapestry needle and white, sew one flower over ch-4 sp at base of each pineapple on rnd 14 of Doily. ❑❑

Winter Roses

Design by Agnes Russell

SKILL LEVEL
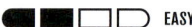 EASY

FINISHED SIZE
17½ inches in diameter

MATERIALS
- J. & P. Coats Metallic size 10 crochet cotton:
    350 yds #1S white/silver
    75 yds ##126S scarlet/silver
- Aunt Lydia's size 10 crochet cotton:
    75 yds #484 myrtle green
- Size 7/1.65mm steel crochet hook or size needed to obtain gauge

GAUGE
3 shell rnds = 1 inch

SPECIAL STITCHES
Beginning shell (beg shell): Sl st across to ch sp, (ch 3, dc, ch 3, 2 dc) in ch sp.
Shell: (2 dc, ch 3, 2 dc) in next st or ch sp.
Beginning double shell (beg dbl shell): (Ch 3, dc, ch 3, 2 dc, ch 3, 2 dc) in st or ch sp.
Double shell (dbl shell): (2 dc, ch 3, 2 dc, ch 3, 2 dc) in next st or ch sp.

INSTRUCTIONS
DOILY
Rnd 1: With white/silver cotton, ch 5, sl st in first ch to form ring, ch 3 (*counts as first dc*), dc in ring, ch 3, [2 dc in ring, ch 3] 7 times, join with sl st in top of beg ch-3.
Rnd 2: Beg shell (*see Special Stitches*), shell (*see Special Stitches*) in each of next 7 ch-3 sps, join with sl st in top of ch-3 of beg shell.
Rnd 3: Beg shell, ch 4, [shell in ch sp of next shell, ch 4] around, join. Fasten off.
Rnd 4: Join myrtle green with sl st in any ch-3 sp of shell, (ch 3, dc, ch 3, 2 dc) in same ch sp, ch

2, [dc in next ch-4 sp, ch 2] 6 times, *shell in shell, ch 2, [dc in ch-4 sp, ch 2] 6 times, rep from * around, join, pull up a lp of myrtle green, remove hook, **do not fasten off.**
Rnd 5: *Join scarlet/silver with sl st in second ch-2 sp to the left of shell, ch 1, (sc, 6 dc, sc) in ch-2 sp, (sc, 6 dc, sc) in each of next 4 ch-2 sps, pull up a lp, remove hook, insert hook in first sc of first petal, pick up dropped lp and pull through st on hook, ch 1, fasten off, rep from * 7 more times. (*8 flowers*)
Rnd 6: Pick up dropped lp of myrtle green, beg shell in shell, [ch 5, sc in next ch-2 sp] twice, ch 5, *shell in shell, [ch 5, sc in next ch-2 sp] twice, ch 5, rep from * around, join. Fasten off.
Rnd 7: Join white/silver with sl st in any ch-3 sp of shell, (ch 3, dc, ch 3, 2 dc) in same ch sp, [ch 3, sc in next ch-5 sp] 3 times, ch 3, *shell in shell, [ch 3, sc in next ch-5 sp] 3 times, ch 3, rep from * around, join.
Rnd 8: Beg dbl shell (*see Special Stitches*) in shell, [ch 3, sc in next ch-3 sp] 4 times, ch 3, *dbl shell (*see Special Stitches*) in shell, [ch 3, sc in next ch-3 sp] 4 times, ch 3, rep from * around, join.
Row 9 (RS): Beg shell in shell in first ch sp of dbl shell, ch 2, shell in next ch sp, turn.
Row 10: Beg shell in shell, ch 2, 5 dc in ch-2 sp, ch 2, shell in shell, turn.
Row 11: Beg shell in shell, ch 2, dc in first dc of 5-dc group, [ch 1, dc in next dc] 4 times, ch 2, shell in shell, turn.
Row 12: Beg shell in shell, ch 2, sc in next ch-1 sp, [ch 3, sc in next ch-1 sp] 3 times, ch 2, shell in shell, turn.
Row 13: Beg shell in shell, ch 2, sc in next ch-3 sp, [ch 3, sc in next ch-3 sp] twice, ch 2, shell in shell, turn.
Row 14: Beg shell in shell, ch 2, sc in next ch-3 sp, ch 3, sc in next ch-3

sp, ch 2, shell in shell, turn.
Row 15: Beg shell in shell, ch 2, sc in next ch-3 sp, ch 2, shell in shell, turn.
Row 16: Beg dbl shell in shell, ch 2, dbl shell in shell, turn.
Row 17: Dbl shell in shell, ch 2, [shell in shell, ch 2] twice, dbl shell in shell, turn.
Row 18: Beg shell in shell, [ch 2, shell in shell] 5 times. Fasten off.
Next rows: *With finished pineapple to the right, join white with sl st in first ch-3 sp of dbl shell, rep rows 9–18, rep from * 6 more times. *(8 pineapples)*
At the end of last pineapple rep, turn, **do not fasten off**.
Note: On the rem rnds and rows of doily, pattern will indicate to shell in shell; if it is the first shell of a rnd, simply work beg shell in first ch-3 sp.
Rnd 19: Sl st into ch-3 sp of shell, *shell in shell, ch 2, 5 dc in next ch-3 sp of shell, ch 2, [shell in shell, ch 2] twice, 5 dc in ch-3 sp of shell, ch 2, shell in shell, ch 2, working across next 6-shell section, rep from * across, continue to rep across each section until all 8 sections are completed, join.
Rnd 20: *Shell in shell, ch 2, dc in first dc of 5-dc group, [ch 1, dc in next dc] 4 times, ch 2, shell in shell, ch 2, rep from * around, join.
Rnd 21: *Shell in shell, ch 2, sc in next ch-1 sp, [ch 3, sc in next ch-1 sp] 3 times, ch 2, shell in shell, ch 2, rep from * around, join.
Row 22 (RS): Shell in shell, ch 2, sc in next ch-3 sp, [ch 3, sc in next ch-3 sp] twice, ch 2, shell in shell, turn.
Row 23 (WS): Shell in shell, ch 2, sc in next ch-3 sp, ch 3, sc in next ch-3 sp, ch 2, shell in shell, turn.
Row 24 (RS): Shell in shell, ch 2, sc in rem ch-3 sp, ch 2, shell in shell, turn.
Row 25 (WS): [Shell in shell] twice. Fasten off.
Next rows: *With finished pineapple to the right, join white with sl st in next free ch-3 sp of shell, rep rows 22–25, rep from * around.
At the end of the 16th pineapple, turn, **do not fasten off**.

TRIM
Rnd 26 (RS): Sl st into ch-3 sp of shell, ch 1, *sc in ch-3 sp of shell, ch 4, sc in next ch-3 sp of shell, [ch 4, sc over dc at side edge of shell] 4 times, ch 4, sc over ch-2 sp, [ch 4, sc over dc at side edge of shell] 4 times, ch 4, rep from * around entire outer edge, join with sl st in beg sc. Fasten off.
Rnd 27 (RS): Join myrtle green with sl st in any ch-4 sp, (ch 1, sc, ch 3, dc) in same ch-4 sp, (sc, ch 3, dc) in each ch-4 sp around, join. Fasten off.❏❏

Pinks & Pineapples Doily

Design by Emma Willey

SKILL LEVEL
 EASY

FINISHED SIZE
23 inches across

MATERIALS
❏ Size 10 crochet cotton:
   325 yds white
   175 yds dusty rose
❏ Size 6/1.80mm steel crochet hook or size needed to obtain gauge

GAUGE
Rnds 1 and 2 = 1¾ inches across

PATTERN NOTE
This project may ruffle until blocked.

SPECIAL STITCHES
Shell: (2 dc, ch 1, 2 dc) in next ch sp.
Beginning shell (beg shell): (Ch 3—*counts as first dc,* dc, ch 1, 2 dc) in specified ch sp.
Picot: Ch 3, sl st in third ch from hook.

INSTRUCTIONS

DOILY

Rnd 1: With dusty rose, ch 6, sl st in first ch to form ring, ch 3 *(counts as first dc)*, 2 dc in ring, ch 3, [3 dc in ring, ch 3] 5 times, join with sl st in top of ch-3. *(18 dc, 6 ch-3 sps)*

Rnd 2: Ch 3, **dc dec** *(see Stitch Guide)* in next 2 sts, ch 3, dc in next ch-3 sp, ch 3, [dc dec in next 3 sts, ch 3, dc in next ch-3 sp, ch 3] around, join. Fasten off. *(12 ch-3 sps)*

Rnd 3: Join white with sc in first ch-3 sp, ch 5, [sc in next ch-3 sp, ch 5] around, join with sl st in beg sc.

Rnd 4: Ch 3, (3 dc, ch 3, 3 dc) in next ch-5 sp, *dc in next st, (3 dc, ch 3, 3 dc) in next ch-5 sp; rep from * around, join with sl st in top of beg ch-3.

Rnd 5: Sl st in each of next 3 sts, sl st in next ch-3 sp, ch 3, 6 dc in same ch sp, ch 2, **shell** *(see Special Stitches)* in next ch-3 sp, ch 2, [7 dc in next ch-3 sp, ch 2, shell in next ch-3 sp, ch 2] around, join. *(42 dc, 12 ch-2 sps, 6 shells)*

Rnd 6: Ch 4 *(counts as first dc and ch 1)*, dc in next dc, [ch 1, dc in next dc] 5 times, *ch 1, sk next ch-2 sp, shell in ch-1 sp of next shell, ch 1, sk next ch-2 sp**, dc in next dc, [ch 1, dc in next dc] 6 times; rep from * around, ending last rep at **, join with sl st in third ch of ch-4. *(48 ch-1 sps, 6 shells)*

Rnd 7: Sl st in first ch-1 sp, ch 1, sc in same ch sp, *[ch 4, sc in next ch-1 sp] 5 times, ch 2, shell in next shell, ch 2, sk next ch-1 sp**, sc in next ch-1 sp; rep from * around, ending last rep at **, join with sl st in beg sc.

Rnd 8: Sl st in each of next 2 chs, ch 1, sc in same ch sp, *[ch 4, sc in next ch-4 sp] 4 times, ch 3, (2 dc, ch 1, 2 dc, ch 1, 2 dc) in next shell, ch 3, sk next ch-2 sp**, sc in next ch-4 sp, rep from * around, ending at **, join.

Rnd 9: Sl st in each of next 2 chs, ch 1, sc in same sp, *[ch 4, sc in next ch-4 sp] 3 times, ch 2, sk next ch-3 sp, shell in next ch-1 sp, ch 3, shell in next ch-1 sp, ch 2, sk next ch-3 sp**, sc in next ch-4 sp, rep from * around, ending last rep at **, join.

Rnd 10: Sl st in each of next 2 chs, ch 1, sc in same ch sp, *[ch 4, sc in next ch-4 sp] twice, ch 2, shell in next shell, ch 5, sc in next ch-3 sp, ch 5, shell in next shell, ch 2, sk next ch-2 sp**, sc in next ch-4 sp, rep from * around, ending last rep at ** join.

Rnd 11: Sl st in each of next 2 chs, ch 1, sc in same ch sp, *ch 5, sc in next ch-4 sp, ch 2, shell in next shell, ch 5, [sc in next ch-5 sp, ch 5] twice, shell in next shell, ch 2, sk next ch-2 sp**, sc in next ch-4 sp, rep from * around, ending last rep at **, join.

Rnd 12: Sl st in each of next 3 chs, ch 1, sc in same ch sp, *ch 2, shell in next shell, ch 5, [sc in next ch-5 sp, ch 5] 3 times, shell in next shell, ch 2, sk next ch-2 sp**, sc in next ch-5 sp, rep from * around, ending last rep at **, join.

Rnd 13: Ch 4, *shell in next shell, ch 6, [sc in next ch-5 sp, ch 6] 4 times, shell in next shell, ch 1**, dc in next sc, ch 1, rep from * around, ending last rep at **, join with sl st in third ch of ch-4.

Rnd 14: Sl st in next ch-1 sp, sl st in each of next 2 sts, sl st in next ch-1 sp, **beg shell** *(see Special Stitches)*, *ch 6, [sc in next ch-6 sp, ch 6] 5 times, shell in next shell, ch 1**, shell in next shell; rep from * around, ending last rep at **, join with sl st in top of ch-3, **turn**, sl st into last ch-1 sp made, turn.

Rnd 15: Beg shell, ch 6, [sc in next ch-6 sp, ch 6] 6 times, *shell in next ch-1 sp between shells, ch 6, [sc in next ch-6 sp, ch 6] 6 times, rep from * around, join.

Rnd 16: Sl st in each st and in each ch across to next ch-6 sp, sl st in each of next 3 chs, ch 1, sc in same ch sp, ch 7, [sc in next ch-6 sp, ch 7] around, join with sl st in beg sc. Fasten off. *(42 ch-7 lps)*

First Motif

Rnd 1: With dusty rose, ch 6, sl st in first ch to form ring, ch 3 *(counts as first dc)*, 2 dc in ring, ch 3, [3 dc in ring, ch 3] 5 times, join with sl st in top of ch-3. *(18 dc, 6 ch-3 sps)*

Rnd 2: Ch 3, dc dec in next 2 sts, ch 3, dc in next ch-3 sp, ch 3, [dc dec in next 3 sts, ch 3, dc in next ch-3 sp, ch 3] around, join. Fasten off. *(12 ch-3 sps)*

Rnd 3: Join white with sc in any ch-3 sp, [ch 5, sc in next ch-3 sp] 10 times, ch 2, sc in any ch-7 sp on Doily, ch 2, sc in next ch-3 sp on this motif, ch 2, sc in next ch-7 sp on Doily, ch 2, join with sl st in first sc. Fasten off.

Next Motif

Rnd 1: With dusty rose, ch 6, sl st in first ch to form ring, ch 3, 2 dc in ring, ch 3, [3 dc in ring, ch 3] 5 times, join with sl st in top of ch-3. *(18 dc, 6 ch-3 sps)*

Rnd 2: Ch 3, dc dec in next 2 sts, ch 3, dc in next ch-3 sp, ch 3, [dc dec in next 3 sts, ch 3, dc in next ch-3 sp, ch 3] around, join. Fasten off. *(12 ch-3 sps)*

Note: *For right-handed crocheters: motifs are joined to the right of previous motifs. For left-handed crocheters: motifs are joined to the left of previous motifs.*

Rnd 3: Join white with sc in any ch-3 sp, [ch 5, sc in next ch-3 sp] 7 times, ch 2, sc in third ch-5 sp of previous motif, ch 2, sc in next ch-3 sp on this motif, ch 2, sc in second ch-5 sp on previous motif, ch 2, sc in next ch-3 sp on this motif, ch 5, sc in next ch-3 sp, ch 2, sk next ch-7 sp on Doily after last joining, sc in next ch-7 sp, ch 2, sc in last ch-3 sp on this motif, ch 2, sc in next ch-7 sp on Doily, ch 2, join with sl st in first sc. Fasten off.

Rep next motif 11 more times for a total of 13 motifs.

Last Motif

Rnd 1: With dusty rose, ch 6, sl st in first ch to form ring, ch 3, 2 dc in ring, ch 3, [3 dc in ring, ch 3] 5 times, join with sl st in top of ch-3. *(18 dc, 6 ch-3 sps)*

Rnd 2: Ch 3, dc dec in next 2 sts, ch 3, dc in next ch-3 sp, ch 3, [dc dec in next 3 sts, ch 3, dc in next ch-3 sp, ch 3] around, join. Fasten off. *(12 ch-3 sps)*

Rnd 3: Join white with sc in any ch-3 sp, ch 5, sc in next ch-3 sp, ch 2, sc in ninth ch-5 sp of First Motif, ch 2, sc in next ch-3 sp on this motif, ch 2, sc in eighth ch-5 sp of First Motif, ch 2, sc in next ch-3 sp on this motif, [ch 5, sc in next ch-3 sp] 4 times, ch 2, sc in third ch-5 sp of previous motif, ch 2, sc in next ch-3 sp on this motif, ch 2, sc in second ch-5 sp on previous motif, ch 2, sc in next ch-3 sp on this motif, ch 5, sc in next ch-3 sp, ch 2, sk next ch-7 sp on Doily after last joining, sc in next ch-7 sp, ch 2, sc in last ch-3 sp on this motif, ch 2, sc in next ch-7 sp on Doily, ch 2, join with sl st in first sc. Fasten off.

Border

Rnd 1: Working around entire outer edge of motifs, join white with sc in first ch-5 sp after any joining, [ch 7, sc in next ch-5 sp] 3 times, ch 9, sk next joining, *sc in next ch-5 sp, [ch 7, sc in next ch-5 sp] 3 times, ch 9, sk next joining, rep from * around, join with sl st in beg sc. *(42 ch-7 lps, 14 ch-9 lps)*

Rnd 2: Sl st in each of next 3 chs, beg shell, *ch 5, sc in next ch-7 sp, ch 5, shell in next ch-7 sp, ch 2, 11 dc in next ch-9 sp, ch 2**, shell in next ch-7 sp, rep from * around, ending last rep at **, join with sl st in top of ch-3.

Rnd 3: Sl st in next st, sl st in next ch sp, beg shell, *ch 2, sc in next ch-5 sp, ch 3, sc in next ch-5 sp, ch 2, shell in next shell, ch 1, sk next ch-2 sp, dc in next dc, [ch 1, dc in next dc] 10 times, ch 1, sk next ch-2 sp**, shell in next shell, rep from * around, ending last rep at **, join.

Rnd 4: Sl st in next st, sl st in next ch sp, beg shell, *ch 3, sk next ch-2 sp, (sc, **picot**—*see Special Stitches*) in next ch-3 sp, ch 3, sk next ch-2 sp, shell in next shell, ch 2, sk next ch-1 sp, sc in next ch-1 sp, [ch 4, sc in next ch-1 sp] 9 times, ch 2**, shell in next shell, rep from * around, ending last rep at **, join. Fasten off.

Row 5: Working in rows; for **first pineapple,** join white with sl st in second shell, beg shell, ch 2, sc in next ch-4 sp, [ch 4, sc in next ch-4 sp] 8 times, ch 2, shell in next shell leaving remaining sts unworked, turn. *(8 ch-4 lps, 2 shells)*

Rows 6–12: Ch 5, shell in first shell, ch 2, sc in next ch-4 sp, [ch 4, sc in next ch-4 sp] across to last shell, ch 2, shell in last shell, turn, ending with 2 shells and one ch-4 sp in last row.

Row 13: Ch 5, shell in first shell, ch 2, sc in next ch-4 sp, ch 2, shell in last shell, turn. *(2 shells, 1 sc)*

Row 14: Ch 5, shell in first shell, dc in next sc, shell in last shell, turn.

Row 15: Ch 5, sk first shell, shell in center dc between shells, ch 5, sl st in top of last dc on last shell. Fasten off.

For **next pineapple,** sk next 2 ch-3 sps on rnd 4, join white with sl st in next shell, rep rows 5–15.

Rep **next pineapple** 12 more times around Doily for a total of 14 pineapples.❏❏

Pineapples With Blue Flowers

Design by Maggie Petsch

SKILL LEVEL
■■■□ INTERMEDIATE

FINISHED SIZE
14½ x 10 inches

MATERIALS
- DMC Cebelia size 10 crochet cotton (282 yds per ball): 1 ball white (MC)
- DMC Cebelia size 20 crochet cotton (405 yds per ball): 1 ball each #743 dark yellow (A), #800 light blue (B) and #799 dark blue (C)
- Size 8/1.50mm steel crochet hook or size needed to obtain gauge
- Size 7/1.65mm steel crochet hook

GAUGE
Size 8 hook and 20 thread: Rnds 1–7 of Flower Motif = 1⅛ inches in diameter

SPECIAL STITCH
Shell: (3 dc, ch 2, 3 dc) in indicated st or ch sp.

INSTRUCTIONS
FIRST PINEAPPLE STRIP
First Pineapple

Row 1 (RS): With size 7 hook and MC, ch 10, sl st in first ch to form ring, *(ch 4, 3 dc, ch 2, 2 dc, ch 2, 3 dc) in ring*, ch 4, sl st in ring, rep from * to * once, tr in ring, turn.

Row 2: Ch 4, **shell** (see Special Stitch) in next ch-2 sp, ch 3, shell in next ch-2 sp, tr in next ch-4 sp, turn.

Row 3: Ch 4, shell in ch sp of next shell, ch 2, (dc, ch 3, dc) in next ch-3 sp, ch 2, shell in next shell, tr in next ch-4 sp, turn.

Row 4: Ch 4, shell in next shell, ch 2, 9 dc in next ch-3 sp, ch 2, shell in next shell, tr in next ch-4 sp, turn.

Row 5: Ch 4, shell in next shell, ch 2, sk next ch-2 sp, dc in next dc, [ch 1, dc in next dc] 8 times, ch 2, shell in next shell, tr in next ch-4 sp, turn.

Row 6: Ch 4, shell in next shell, ch 4, sc in next ch-1 sp, [ch 3, sc in next ch-1 sp] 7 times, ch 4, shell in next shell, tr in next ch-4 sp, turn.

Row 7: Ch 4, shell in next shell, ch 4, sc in next ch-3 sp, [ch 3, sc in next ch-3 sp] 6 times, ch 4, shell in next shell, tr in next ch-4 sp, turn.

Row 8: Ch 4, shell in next shell, ch 4, sc in next ch-3 sp, [ch 3, sc in next ch-3 sp] 5 times, ch 4, shell in next shell, tr in next ch-4 sp, turn.

Row 9: Ch 4, shell in next shell, ch 4, sc in next ch-3 sp, [ch 3, sc in next ch-3 sp] 4 times, ch 4, shell in next shell, tr in next ch-4 sp, turn.

Row 10: Ch 4, shell in next shell, ch 4, sc in next ch-3 sp, [ch 3, sc in next ch-3 sp] 3 times, ch 4, shell in next shell, tr in next ch-4 sp, turn.

Row 11: Ch 4, shell in next shell, ch 4, sc in next ch-3 sp, [ch 3, sc in next ch-3 sp] twice, ch 4, shell in next shell, tr in next ch-4 sp, turn.

Row 12: Ch 4, shell in next shell, ch 4, sc in next ch-3 sp, ch 3, sc in next ch-3 sp, ch 4, shell in next shell, tr in next ch-4 sp, turn.

Row 13: Ch 4, shell in next shell, ch 4, sc in next ch-3 sp, ch 4, shell in next shell, tr in next ch-4 sp, turn.

Row 14: Ch 4, [shell in next shell] twice, tr in next ch-4 sp, turn.

Row 15: Ch 5, holding back on hook last lp of each st, tr in ch sp of next shell, dtr between shells, tr in ch sp of next shell, dtr in next ch-4 sp, yo, pull through all lps on hook. Fasten off.

Second Pineapple
Row 2: With WS facing, join thread with sl st in next ch-4 sp on row 1, rep row 2 of First Pineapple.
Rows 3–15: Rep rows 3–15 of First Pineapple.

REMAINING THREE PINEAPPLE STRIPS
First Pineapple
Rows 1–7: Rep rows 1–7 of First Pineapple for First Pineapple Strip.
Row 8: Ch 4, shell in next shell, ch 4, sc in next ch-3 sp, [ch 3, sc in next ch-3 sp] 5 times, ch 4, shell in next shell, yo twice, with previous Pineapple Strip to left of working strip, WS facing, insert hook in end sp before last shell on row 8 of top pineapple on previous strip, yo, pull through sp and 2 lps on hook, yo, pull through 2 lps on hook, turn.
Rows 9–15: Rep rows 9–15 of First Pineapple for First Pineapple strip.

Second Pineapples
Row 2: With WS facing, join thread with sl st in next ch-4 sp on row 1, rep row 2 of First Pineapple.
Rows 3–7: Rep rows 3–7 of First Pineapple for First Pineapple Strip.
Row 8: Ch 2, sl st in end sp before end shell on row 8 of corresponding pineapple on previous Pineapple Strip, ch 1, shell in next shell on working strip, continue across as for row 8 of First Pineapple for First Pineapple Strip.
Rows 9–15: Rep rows 9–15 of First Pineapple for First Pineapple Strip.

FLOWER MOTIF
Make 3.
Rnd 1 (RS): With size 8 hook and A, ch 2, 6 sc in second ch from hook, join with sl st in beg sc.
Rnd 2: Ch 4 (*counts as first hdc, ch-2*), [hdc in next sc, ch 2] around, join with sl st in second ch of beg ch-4. Fasten off. (*6 ch-2 sps*)
Rnd 3: With size 8 hook, join B with sl st in any ch-2 sp, ch 1, (sc, 3 dc, sc) in same sp and in each ch-2 sp around, **do not join.** (*6 petals*)
Rnd 4: Working behind petals of last rnd, sc in second ch of beg ch-2 of rnd 2, ch 3, [sc in sk hdc of rnd 2, ch 3] around, join with sl st in beg sc.
Rnd 5: (Sc, 5 dc, sc) in each ch-3 sp around, **do not join.** (*6 petals*)
Rnd 6: Working behind petals of last rnd, sc in beg sc of rnd 4, ch 4, [sc in next sk sc of rnd 4, ch 4] around, join.
Rnd 7: (Sc, 7 dc, sc) in each ch-4 sp around, **do not join.** (*6 petals*)
Rnd 8: Working behind petals of last rnd, sl st in beg sc of rnd 6, ch 5, [sl st in next sk sc of rnd 6, ch 5] around, join with sl st in beg sl st. Fasten off.
Rnd 9: With RS facing, with size 8 hook, join A with sl st in any ch-5 sp, ch 1, sc in same ch sp, [ch 7, (sc, ch 7, sc) in next ch sp] around, ending with ch 7, sc in same ch sp as beg sc, ch 7, join. Fasten off. (*12 ch-7 sps*)

JOINING BETWEEN FIRST TWO PINEAPPLE STRIPS
Rnd 10: With RS facing and size 8 hook, join C with sl st in fourth ch of any ch-7 sp of last rnd, ch 5, sl st over end st on row 7 of pineapple in upper right-hand corner, ch 3, sl st over end st on row 7 of pineapple in upper left-hand corner, ch 5, sl st in same ch of first ch-7 sp of Flower Motif as beg sl st, *[ch 3, sl st over end st on next row of pineapple, ch 3, sl st in fourth ch of next ch-7 sp of Flower Motif] 3 times*, ch 4, sl st over end st on next row of pineapple, ch 5, sl st over end st on row 3 of next pineapple, ch 4, sl st in same ch of ch-7 sp of Flower Motif, rep from * to * once **, ch 5, sl st over end st on next row of pineapple, ch 3, sl st over end st on row 7 of next pineapple, ch 5, sl st in same ch of ch-7 sp of Flower Motif, rep from * around, ending last rep at **. Fasten off.

Make and join two more Flower Motifs to rem two center sps between Pineapple Strips.

Small Flower
Rnd 1: With size 8 hook and A, ch 2, 6 sc in second ch from hook, join with sl st in beg sc. Fasten off.

Joining
Rnd 2: With size 8 hook, join B with sl st in any sc of rnd 1, ch 2, dc in same st, sl st over end st of row 10 on left edge of bottom pineapple on First Pineapple Strip to the right, *dc in same st on Small Flower as last dc, ch 2, (sl st, ch 2, dc) in next sc on Small Flower, sl st over end st on next row of pineapple, dc in same sc on Small Flower as last dc, ch 2*, (sl st, ch 2, dc) in next sc on Small Flower, sl st over end st on row 9 of next pineapple, rep from * to * once, [(sl st, ch 2, 2 dc, ch 2) in next sc on Small Flower] twice, join with sl st in beg sl st. Fasten off.

Make five more Small Flowers, joining to rem two sps between Pineapple Strips across bottom of doily and in three sps across top of doily.

Make two more Small Flowers, joining four petals on each as for first six Small Flowers over end sts of rows 3 and 2 between top and bottom pineapples on each end Pineapple Strip.

BORDER
Rnd 1: With RS facing and size 8 hook, join A with sl st in top of last st of row 15 on top pineapple of First Pineapple Strip at right-hand side of doily, ch 1, (sc, ch 7, sc) in same st, *ch 5, sc over end sp of same row, [ch 5, sc over end sp of next row] 3 times, ch 7, sc at tip of first free petal on Small Flower, ch 7, sc in tip of next free petal, ch 7, sc over end sp on row 12 of next Pineapple Strip, [ch 5, sc over end sp on next row] 3 times, ch 5, (sc, ch 7, sc) in top of st at

tip of same pineapple, rep from * across to tip of last Pineapple Strip at next corner, ch 5, sc over end sp of same row of same Pineapple Strip, [ch 5, sc over end sp of next row] 10 times, [ch 7, sc at tip of next free petal on Small Flower] twice, ch 7, sc over end sp on row 5 of next pineapple, [ch 5, sc over end sp of next row] 10 times, ch 5**, (sc, ch 7, sc) in top of st at tip of same pineapple, rep from * around, ending last rep at **, join. Fasten off.

Rnd 2: With size 8 hook and RS facing, join C with sl st in fourth ch of ch-7 sp at tip of first pineapple in upper right-hand corner, ch 8 *(counts as first dtr, ch-3)*, dtr in same ch, ◊*ch 5, tr in third ch of next ch-5 sp, [ch 5, dc in third ch of next ch-5 sp] 3 times, ch 5, dc in third ch of next ch-7 sp, ch 3, dc in fourth ch of next ch-7 sp, ch 3, dc in fifth ch of next ch-7 sp, [ch 5, dc in third ch of next ch-5 sp] 3 times, ch 5, tr in third ch of next ch-5 sp, ch 5, (dtr, ch 3, dtr) in fourth ch of next ch-7 sp, rep from * across to last ch-7 sp at tip of pineapple in next corner, ch 5, tr in third ch of next ch-5 sp, [ch 5, dc in third ch of next ch-5 sp] 10 times, ch 5, dc in third ch of next ch-7 sp, ch 3, sk next 3 chs, hdc in next ch, ch 3, sc in fourth ch of next ch-7 sp, ch 3, hdc in first ch of next ch-7 sp, ch 3, sk next 3 chs, dc in next ch, [ch 5, dc in third ch of next ch-5 sp] 10 times, ch 5, tr in third ch of next ch-5 sp, ch 5**, (dtr, ch 3, dtr) in fourth ch of next ch-7 sp, rep from ◊ around, ending last rep at **, join with sl st in fifth ch of beg ch-8. Fasten off.

Rnd 3: With RS facing and size 7 hook, join MC with sl st in ch-3 sp at upper right corner, ch 1, (sc, ch 5, sc) in same ch sp, * [ch 5, sc in next ch sp] 5 times, ch 5, sk next ch sp, sc in next dc, ch 5, sk next ch sp, [sc in next ch sp, ch 5] 5 times, (sc, ch 5, sc) in next ch-3 sp, rep from * across to next corner ch-3 sp, [ch 5, sc in next ch sp] 13 times sc in next ch sp, ch 3, [sc in next ch sp] twice, ch 5, [sc in next ch sp, ch 5] 12 times**, (sc, ch 5, sc) in next ch-3 sp, rep from * around, ending last rep at **, join.

Rnd 4: Sl st in each of next 3 chs, ch 1, sc in same ch sp, [ch 5, sc in next ch sp] 6 times, *[sc in next ch sp, {ch 5, sc in next ch sp} 12 times] twice, sc in next ch sp*, [ch 5, sc in next ch sp] 40 times, rep from * to *, [ch 5, sc in next ch sp] 33 times, ch 5, join.

Rnd 5: Sl st in each of next 3 chs, [ch 3, (2 dc, ch 3, 2 dc) in next ch-2 sp, sl st in third ch of next ch-5 sp] 5 times, sl st in third ch of next ch-5 sp, *rep between [ ] 11 times, sl st in third ch of next ch-5 sp*, rep from * to * once, **rep between [ ] 19 times, sl st in third ch of next ch-5 sp**, rep from ** to ** once, rep from * to * twice, rep from ** to ** once, rep between [ ] 14 times, join. Fasten off.❑❑

Petite Pineapples

Design by Maggie Petsch

SKILL LEVEL
■■■□ EXPERIENCED

FINISHED SIZE
9 x 15¾ inches

MATERIALS
- ❑ DMC Cebelia crochet cotton size 20 (50g per ball):
  1 ball white *(MC)*
- ❑ DMC pearl cotton size 8 (10g per ball):
  1 ball #48 shaded pink *(A)*
  Small amount #104 shaded yellow *(B)*
- ❑ Size 8/1.50mm steel crochet hook or size needed to obtain gauge
- ❑ Sewing needle
- ❑ White sewing thread

GAUGE
2 blocks over a bar and 1 lacet = 1 inch; rows 1–5 = 1 inch
Flower = 1¼ inches in diameter

PATTERN NOTE
When working from chart and graph, read all odd-numbered (right side) rows from right to left, all even-numbered (wrong side) rows from left to right.

SPECIAL STITCHES
Beginning 2-block increase (beg inc): Ch 8, dc in fourth ch from hook and in each of next 4 chs, dc in next dc.

End 2-block increase (end inc): Fdc in last st of row, [fdc in base of last fdc made] 6 times.

Foundation dc (fdc): Yo, insert hook in indicated st or sp, yo, pull up a lp, yo, pull through 1 lp on hook *(base made)*, [yo, pull through 2 lps on hook] twice.

Block: Dc in each of next 3 sts, or 2 dc in ch-2 sp, dc in next dc.

Double block: 5 dc in next bar, dc in next dc.

18 Flower Garden Pineapple Doilies • Annie's Attic, Berne, IN 46711 • AnniesAttic.com

Mesh: Ch 2, sk next 2 sts, dc in next st.

Bar: Ch 5, sk next sc, dc in next dc.

Lacet: Ch 3, sk next 2 sts, sc in next st, ch 3, sk next 2 sts, dc in next st, or ch 3, sk next 2 chs, sc in next ch, ch 3, dc in next dc.

Beginning block (beg block): Ch 3 *(counts as first dc)*, dc in each of next 3 sts.

Beginning lacet (beg lacet): Ch 6 *(counts as first dc, ch 3)*, sk next 2 sts, sc in next st, ch 3, sk next 2 sts, dc in next st.

Beginning bar (beg bar): Ch 8 *(counts as first dc, ch 5)*, dc in next dc.

Beginning V-stitch (beg V-st): (Ch 4 {*counts as first dc, ch 1*}, dc) in indicated st.

V-stitch (V-st): (Dc, ch 1, dc) in indicated st.

Cluster (cl): Holding back on hook last lp of each st, tr in next tr, sk next sp, dc in next sp, tr in next tr, yo, pull through all lps on hook.

Picot: Ch 2, sl st in top of last st made.

INSTRUCTIONS
CENTER

Row 1 (RS): With MC, ch 117, dc in fourth ch from hook and in each of next 5 chs, *ch 3, sk next 2 chs, sc in next ch, ch 3, sk next 2 chs, dc in next ch] 5 times, dc in each of next 6 chs, rep from * across, turn.

Row 2: Work according to graph using Special Stitches as needed, turn.

Row 3: Beg inc *(see Special Stitches)*, *mesh twice, double block, lacet 3 times, double block rep from * twice, mesh twice, **end inc** *(see Special Stitches)*, turn.

Rows 4–11: Work according to graph across, turn.

Row 12: Ch 8, dc in next dc, ch 5, dc in next dc, *dc in each of next 6 dc, [ch 2, dc in next dc] twice, dc in each of next 6 dc**, [ch 2, dc in next dc] twice, 5 dc in next dc, dc in next dc, [ch 2, dc in next dc] twice *(row 1 of Chart)*, rep from * twice, rep from * to ** once, ch 5, dc in next dc, ch 5, dc in third ch of turning ch-6, turn.

Rows 13–26: Work graph and chart as indicated, at end of last row, fasten off.

BORDER
Rnd 1: With RS facing, join A with sl st in last dc of row 26, *ch 7, sk next 5 dc, sl st in next dc**, [ch 7, sl st in next dc] 5 times*, rep from * to * twice, rep from * to ** once, [ch 9, sk next row, sl st in top of end st of next row] 3 times, ch 7, sk same row and next row, sl st over end st of next row, [ch 7, sk next 2 rows, sl st over end st of next row] 3 times, ch 7, sk next row, sl st at base of end st of next row, [ch 9, sk next row, sl st at base of end st of next row] 3 times, working in rem lps across foundation ch at bases of sts of row 1, rep from * to * across to last 6 sts, rep from * to ** once, [ch 9, sk next row, sl st at base of end st of next row] 3 times, ch 7, sk same row and next row, sl st over end st of next row, [ch 7, sk next 2 rows, sl st over end st of next row] 3 times, ch 7, sk next row, sl st in top of end st of next row, [ch 9, sk next row, sl st in top of end st of next row] twice, ch 9, join with sl st in beg sl st. Fasten off. *(60 ch sps)*

Rnd 2: With RS facing, join MC with sl st in center ch of beg ch-7 of last rnd, **beg V-st** *(see Special Stitches)* in same ch, *[ch 3, 5 dc in center ch of next ch sp, ch 3, **V-st** *(see Special Stitches)* in center ch of next ch sp] 9 times, [ch 5, 5 dc in center ch of next ch sp, ch 5, V-st in center ch of next ch sp] twice, [ch 3, 5 dc in center ch of next ch sp, ch 3, V-st in center ch of next ch sp] twice**, [ch 5, 5 dc in center ch of next ch sp, ch 5, V-st in center ch of next ch sp] twice, rep from * around, ending last rep at **, ch 5, 5 dc in center ch of next ch sp, ch 5, V-st in center ch of next ch sp, ch 5, 5 dc in center ch of next ch sp, ch 5, join with sl st in third ch of beg ch-4.

Rnd 3: Ch 4 *(counts as first dc, ch-1 throughout)*, dc in next ch-1 sp, ch 1, dc in next dc, *[ch 1, {dc in next dc, ch 1} 5 times, dc in next dc, ch 1, dc in next ch sp, ch 1, dc in next dc] 9 times, ch 3, [dc in next dc, ch 1] 4 times, dc in next dc, ch 3, dc in next dc, ch 2, dc in next ch sp, ch 2, dc in next dc, ch 3, [dc in next dc, ch 1] 4 times, dc in next dc, ch 3, [dc in next dc, ch 1, dc in next ch sp, ch 1, dc in next dc, ch 1, {dc in next dc, ch 1} 5 times] twice, dc in next dc, ch 1, dc in next ch sp, ch 1, dc in next dc, ch 3, [dc in next dc, ch 1] 4 times, dc in next dc, ch 3, dc in next dc, ch 2, dc in next ch sp, ch 2, dc in next dc, ch 3, [dc in next dc, ch 1] 4 times, dc in next dc, ch 3**, dc in next dc, ch 1, dc in next ch sp, ch 1, dc in next dc, rep from * around, ending last rep at **, join.

Rnd 4: Sl st in next ch and in next dc, ch 4, (dc, ch 1, dc) in same st, *[ch 3, sk next 2 ch-1 sps, {sc in next ch-1 sp, ch 3} 4 times, V-st in center dc of next 3-dc group] 8 times, ch 3, sk next 2 ch-1 sps, [sc in next ch-1 sp, ch 3] 4 times, [{dc, ch 1} twice in center dc of next 3-dc group, dc in same st, ch 5, sk next ch-3 sp, sc in next ch-1 sp, {ch 3, sc in next ch-1 sp} 3 times, ch 5] twice, [V-st in center dc of next 3-dc group, ch 3, sk next 2 ch-1 sps, {sc in next ch-1 sp, ch 3} 4 times] twice, V-st in center dc of next 3-dc group**, [ch 5, sk next ch-3 sp, sc in next ch-1 sp, {ch 3, sc in next ch-1 sp} 3 times, ch 5, {dc, ch 1} twice in center dc of next 3-dc group, dc in same st] twice, rep from * around, ending last rep at **, ch 5, sk next ch-3 sp, sc in next ch-1 sp, [ch 3, sc in next ch-1 sp] 3 times, ch 5, [dc, ch 1] twice in center dc of next 3-dc group, dc in same st, ch 5, sk next ch-3 sp, sc in next ch-1 sp, [ch 3, sc in next ch-1 sp] 3 times, ch 5, join.

Rnd 5: Ch 4, V-st in next dc, ch 1, dc in next dc, *[ch 3, sk next ch-3 sp, {sc in next ch-3 sp, ch 3} 3 times, dc in next dc, ch 1, dc in next ch sp, ch 1, dc in next dc] 8 times, ch 3, sk next ch-3 sp, [sc in next ch-3 sp, ch 3] 3 times, [dc in next dc, ch 1, V-st in next dc, ch 1, dc in next dc, ch 5, sk next ch sp, sc in next ch-3 sp, {ch 3, sc in next ch-3 sp} twice, ch 5] twice, [dc in next dc, ch 1, dc in next ch sp, ch 1, dc in next dc, ch 3, sk next ch-3 sp, {sc in next ch-3 sp, ch 3} 3 times] twice, dc in next dc, ch 1, dc in next ch sp, ch 1, dc in next dc**, [ch 5, sk next ch sp, sc in next ch-3 sp, {ch 3, sc in next ch-3 sp} twice, ch 5, dc in next dc, ch 1, V-st in next dc, ch 1, dc in next dc] twice, rep from * around, ending last rep at **, ch 5, sk next ch sp, sc in next ch-3 sp, {ch 3, sc in next ch-3 sp} twice, ch 5, dc in next dc, ch 1, V-st in next dc, ch 1, dc in next dc, ch 5, sk next ch sp, sc in next ch-3 sp, [ch 3, sc in next ch-3 sp] twice, ch 5, join.

Rnd 6: Ch 6 *(counts as first tr, ch-2 throughout)*, [tr in next ch sp, ch 2, tr in next dc, ch 2] twice, tr in next ch sp, ch 2, tr in next dc, *[ch 3, sk next ch-3 sp, {sc in next ch-3 sp, ch 3} twice, {tr in next dc, ch 2, tr in next ch sp, ch 2} twice, tr in next dc] 8 times, ch 3, sk next ch-3 sp, [sc in next ch-3 sp, ch 3] twice, [{tr in next dc, ch 2, tr in next ch sp, ch 2} 3 times, tr in next dc, ch 5, sc in next ch-3 sp, ch 3, sc in next ch-3 sp, ch 5] twice, [{tr in next dc, ch 2, tr in next ch sp, ch 2} twice, tr in next dc, ch 3, sk next ch sp, {sc in next ch-3 sp, ch 3} twice] twice, [tr in next dc, ch 2, tr in next ch sp, ch 2 twice, tr in next dc**, [ch 5, sc in next ch-3 sp, ch 3, sc in next ch-3 sp, ch 5, {tr in next dc, ch 2, tr in next ch sp, ch 2} 3 times, tr in next dc] twice, rep from * around, ending last rep at **, ch 5, sk next ch sp, sc in next ch-3 sp, ch 3, sc in next ch-3 sp, ch 5, [tr in next dc, ch 2, tr in next ch sp, ch 2] 3 times, tr in next dc, ch 5, sc in next ch-3 sp, ch 3, sc in next ch-3 sp, ch 5, join in fourth ch of beg ch-6.

Rnd 7: Ch 6, sl st in third ch from hook, *[ch 3, tr in next tr, **picot** *(see Special Stitches)*] 5 times, [ch 3, **cl** *(see Special Stitches)*, picot, {ch 3, tr in next tr, picot} 3 times] 8 times, ch 3, cl, picot in cl, [{ch

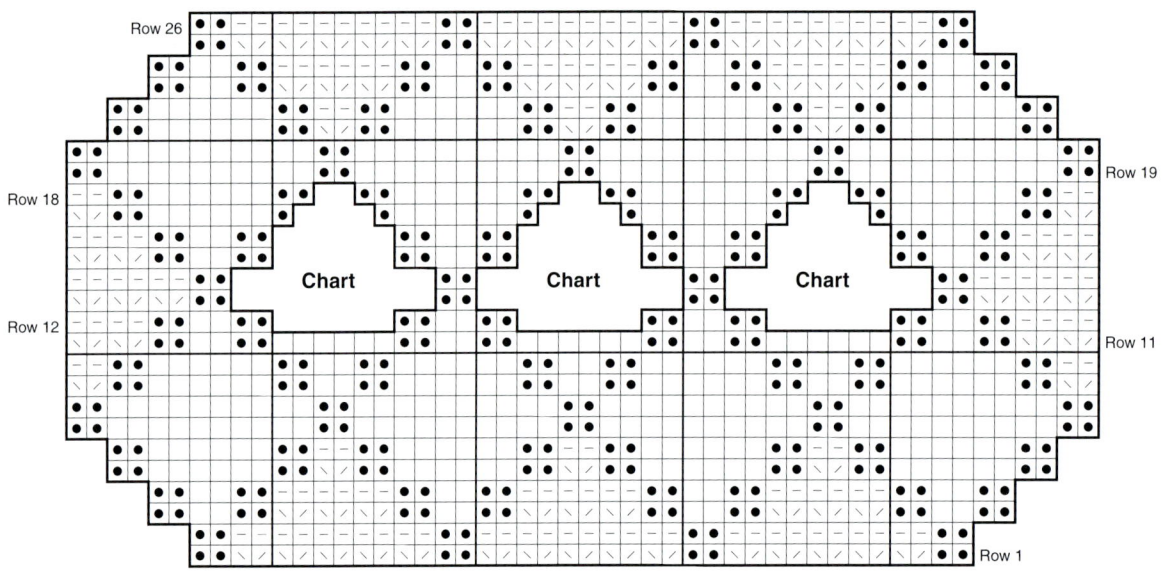

Graph

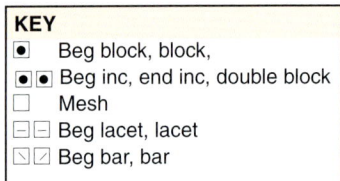

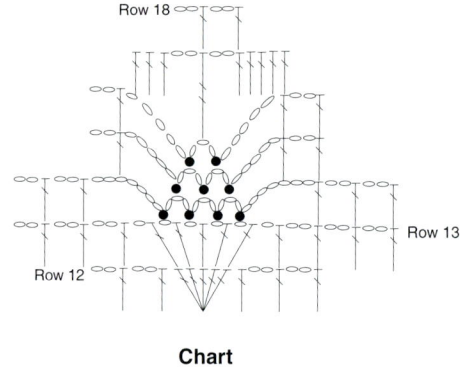

Chart

20 Flower Garden Pineapple Doilies • Annie's Attic, Berne, IN 46711 • AnniesAttic.com

3, tr in next tr, picot} 6 times, ch 1, dc in next ch-3 sp, picot, ch 1, tr in next tr, picot] twice, [{ch 3, tr in next tr, picot} 3 times, [ch 3, cl, picot] twice, [ch 3, tr in next tr, picot] 4 times, ch 1, dc in next ch-3 sp, picot, ch 1, tr in next tr, picot, [ch 3, tr in next tr, picot] 6 times, ch 1, dc in next ch-3 sp, picot, ch 1**, tr in next tr, picot, rep from * around, ending last rep at **, join in fourth ch of beg ch-6. Fasten off.

FLOWERS
Make 8.
Rnd 1: With B, ch 2, 8 sc in second ch from hook, join with sl st in beg sc. Fasten off. *(8 sc)*
Rnd 2: Join A with sl st in any sc, [ch 7, sc in second ch from hook, hdc in next ch, dc in each of next 2 chs, hdc in next ch, sc in next ch, sl st in next st on rnd 1] 8 times. Fasten off.

FINISHING
With sewing needle and thread, tack one Flower at center of each of eight filet mesh diamonds.

Latticework & Lavender
Design by Maggie Petsch

SKILL LEVEL
■■■□ INTERMEDIATE

FINISHED SIZE
13½ inches square

MATERIALS
- J. & P. Coats Knit-Cro-Sheen size 10 crochet cotton (325 yds per ball):
  1 ball white *(MC)*
  Small amounts each blue *(A)*, dark lavender *(B)*, bright violet *(C)* and canary yellow *(D)*
- South Maid crochet cotton size 10 (300 yds per ball):
  1 ball shaded blues #13 *(E)*
- Size 7/1.65mm steel crochet hook or size needed to obtain gauge

GAUGE
8 sc = 1 inch

INSTRUCTIONS
LATTICEWORK
Row 1 (RS): With MC, ch 122, **sc dec** *(see Stitch Guide)* in second and third chs from hook, *sc in each of next 13 chs, 3 sc in next ch, sc in each of next 13 chs**, sc dec in next 3 chs, rep from * across, ending last rep at **, sc dec in last 2 chs. Fasten off. *(121 sts)*
Row 2: With MC, ch 15, with WS facing, sl st in center sc of first 3-sc group on previous row, [ch 29, sl st in center sc of next 3-sc group on previous row] 3 times, ch 16, 2 sc in second ch from hook, *sc in each of next 13 chs, sc dec in next ch, sl st, and next ch, sc in each of next 13 chs**, 3 sc in next ch, rep from * across to last ch, ending last rep at **, 2 sc in last ch, turn. *(121 sts)*
Row 3: Sl st in first sc, [ch 29, sl st in center sc of next 3-sc group] 3 times, ch 29, sl st in last sc, ch 1, turn, sc dec in sl st and next ch, *sc in each of next 13 chs, 3 sc in next ch, sc in each of next 13 chs**, sc dec in next ch, sl st, and next ch, rep from * across to last 2 sts, ending last rep at **, sc dec in last ch and sl st. Fasten off. *(121 sts)*
Rows 4–8: Rep rows 2 and 3 alternately, ending with row 2. At end of last row, fasten off.

FLOWER
Make 24.

Rnd 1 (RS): With D, ch 2, 8 sc in second ch from hook, join with sl st in **front lp** *(see Stitch Guide)* only of beg sc. *(8 sc)*

Rnd 2: Working in front lps only this rnd, [ch 3, sl st in next st] around, ending with ch 3, join with sl st in same st as joining st of rnd 1, fasten off.

Joining to Latticework
Rnd 3: With RS facing and color indicated on illustration for diamond-shaped opening being worked, join thread with sl st in any rem lp of rnd 1, ch 6, sl st in fifth st from any inside corner st in diamond-shaped opening, *sc in last ch made, hdc in next ch, dc in each of next 2 chs, hdc in next ch, sc in next ch, sl st in next rem lp on rnd 1**, ch 6 *, sk next 4 sts on diamond opening, sl st in next st, rep from * to *, sl st in fifth st from next corner st, rep from * around, ending last rep at **. Fasten off. *(8 petals)*

LATTICEWORK EDGING
With RS facing, join E with sl st in first rem lp of foundation ch in upper right corner, ch 1, sc in same st, *sc in each of next 13 sts, dec in 3 sts at base of first "V," sc in each of next 13 sts**, 3 sc in next st at tip of point, rep from * twice, then rep from * to ** once, 2 sc in next st at tip of point, sc in first st on next edge, sc in each of next 13 sts, sc dec in next st, next joining st between rows and next st on next row at base of next "V," [sc in each of next 14 sts, sc between same row and next row, sc in each of next 14 sts, sc dec in next st, next joining st between rows and next st on next row at base of next "V"] 3 times, sc in each of next 13 sts, 2 sc in next st***, sc in first st on next edge, rep from * around, ending last rep at ***, join with sl st in beg sc. Fasten off.

FIRST SIDE OF PINEAPPLE BORDER
First Pineapple
Row 1: With RS facing, join MC with sl st in third st to the right of sc dec at the base of first "V" at the left corner of any side on Latticework Edging, ch 1, dc in sc dec, ch 1, sk next 2 sts, sl st in next st, ch 3, sk 2 sts, sl st in next st leaving rem sts unworked, turn.

Row 2: Ch 1, (dc, ch 2, dc) in next dc, ch 1, sk next 2 sts on opposite edge, sl st in next st, ch 3, sk next 2 sts, sl st in next st, turn.

Row 3: Ch 2, 6 dc in next ch-2 sp, ch 2, sk next 2 sts on opposite edge, sl st in next st, ch 3, sk next 2 sts, sl st in next st, turn.

Row 4: Ch 2, dc in next dc, [ch 1, dc in next dc] 5 times, ch 2, sk next 2 sts on opposite edge, sl st in next st, ch 3, sk next 2 sts, sl st in next st, turn.

Row 5: Ch 8 *(counts as first dc, ch-5 throughout)*, sc in next dc,

COLOR KEY
A Blue
B Dark lavender
C Bright violet
D Canary yellow
E Shaded blues

[ch 3, sc in next dc] 5 times, ch 5, sk next 2 sts on opposite side, dc in next st, turn.

Row 6: Ch 7 *(counts as first dc, ch-4 throughout)*, sc in next ch-3 sp, [ch 3, sc in next ch-3 sp] 4 times, ch 4, dc in third ch of turning ch-8, turn.

Row 7: Ch 7, sc in next ch-3 sp, [ch 3, sc in next ch-3 sp] 3 times, ch 4, dc in third ch of turning ch-7, turn.

Row 8: Ch 7, sc in next ch-3 sp, [ch 3, sc in next ch-3 sp] twice, ch 4, dc in third ch of turning ch-7, turn.

Row 9: Ch 7, sc in next ch-3 sp, ch 3, sc in next ch-3 sp, ch 4, dc in third ch of turning ch-4, turn.

Row 10: Ch 7, sc in ch-3 sp, ch 4, dc in third ch of turning ch-4, turn.

Row 11: Ch 3, holding back on hook last lp of each st, dtr in next sc, dc in third ch of turning ch-7, yo, pull through all lps on hook. Fasten off.

Next Three Pineapples
Row 1: With RS facing, join MC with sl st in third st to the right of dec at the base of next "V" to the right of previous pineapple worked, ch 1, dc in sc dec, ch 1, sk next 2 sts on opposite edge, sl st in next st, ch 3, sk next 2 sts, sl st in next st, turn.

Rows 2–4: Rep rows 2–4 of First Pineapple.

Row 5: Ch 8, sc in next dc, [ch 3, sc in next dc] 5 times, ch 5, sl st in third ch of turning ch-8 on row 5 of previous pineapple, turn.

Rows 6–11: Rep rows 6–11 of First Pineapple.

SECOND–FOURTH SIDES OF PINEAPPLE BORDER
First Pineapple
Rows 1–11: Rep rows 1–11 of First Pineapple for First Side on next unworked side of Latticework Edging to the right of last pineapple made.

Next Three Pineapples
Rows 1–11: Rep rows 1–11 of Next Three Pineapples for First Side, at end of row 11 on last pineapple of last side, do not turn or fasten off.

EDGING
Rnd 1: Sl st over side of last dc made, ch 1, sc over same st, *[ch 4, sc over end st of next row] 5 times, ch 1, sc over end st of row 6 on next pineapple, [ch 4, sc over end st of next row] 5 times, ch 4, sc over end st on opposite side of same row, rep from * twice, [ch 4, sc over end st of next row] 6 times, ch 2, sc over end st of row 5 on next pineapple, [ch 4, sc over end st of next row] 6 times, ch 4**, sc over end st on opposite side of same row, rep from * around, ending last rep at **, join. Fasten off.

Rnd 2: With RS facing, join B with sl st in last ch-4 sp made, ch 1, *(sc, ch 4, sc) in same ch-4 sp at tip of pineapple, [ch 4, sc in next ch-4 sp] 5 times, sc in next ch-4 sp on next pineapple, [ch 4, sc in next ch-4 sp] 4 times, ch 4, rep from * twice, (sc, ch 4, sc) in ch-4 sp at tip of pineapple, [ch 4, sc in next ch-4 sp] 6 times, ch 1, sc in next ch-4 sp on next pineapple, [ch 4, sc in next ch-4 sp] 5 times, ch 4, rep from * around, join. Fasten off.❑❑

Annie's Attic

306 East Parr Road
Berne, IN 46711
© 2005 Annie's Attic

TOLL-FREE ORDER LINE or to request a free catalog (800) LV-ANNIE (800) 582-6643
Customer Service (800) AT-ANNIE (800) 282-6643, **Fax** (800) 882-6643
Visit www.AnniesAttic.com

We have made every effort to ensure the accuracy and completeness of these instructions. We cannot, however, be responsible for human error, typographical mistakes or variations in individual work. Reprinting or duplicating the information, photographs or graphics in this publication by any means, including copy machine, computer scanning, digital photography, e-mail, personal Web site and fax, is illegal. Failure to abide by federal copyright laws may result in litigation and fines.

ISBN: 1-59635-025-3   All rights reserved.   Printed in USA   1 2 3 4 5 6 7 8 9

Stitch Guide

ABBREVIATIONS

beg	begin/beginning
bpdc	back post double crochet
bpsc	back post single crochet
bptr	back post treble crochet
CC	contrasting color
ch	chain stitch
ch-	refers to chain or space previously made (i.e. ch-1 space)
ch sp	chain space
cl	cluster
cm	centimeter(s)
dc	double crochet
dec	decrease/decreases/decreasing
dtr	double treble crochet
fpdc	front post double crochet
fpsc	front post single crochet
fptr	front post treble crochet
g	gram(s)
hdc	half double crochet
inc	increase/increases/increasing
lp(s)	loop(s)
MC	main color
mm	millimeter(s)
oz	ounce(s)
pc	popcorn
rem	remain/remaining
rep	repeat(s)
rnd(s)	round(s)
RS	right side
sc	single crochet
sk	skip(ped)
sl st	slip stitch
sp(s)	space(s)
st(s)	stitch(es)
tog	together
tr	treble crochet
trtr	triple treble
WS	wrong side
yd(s)	yard(s)
yo	yarn over

Chain—ch: Yo, pull through lp on hook.

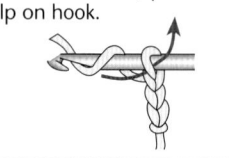

Slip stitch—sl st: Insert hook in st, yo, pull through both lps on hook.

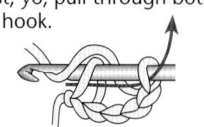

Single crochet—sc: Insert hook in st, yo, pull through st, yo, pull through both lps on hook.

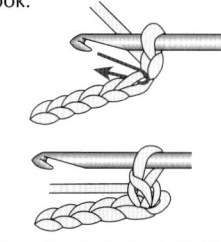

**Front loop—front lp
Back loop—back lp**

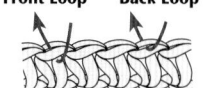

Front post stitch—fp: Back post stitch—bp: When working post st, insert hook from right to left around post st on previous row.

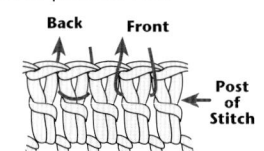

Half double crochet—hdc: Yo, insert hook in st, yo, pull through st, yo, pull through all 3 lps on hook.

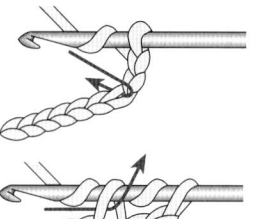

Double crochet—dc: Yo, insert hook in st, yo, pull through st, [yo, pull through 2 lps] twice.

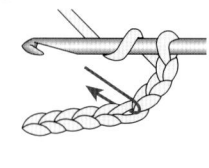
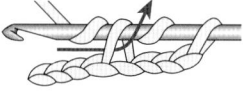
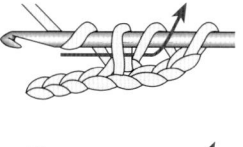

Change colors: Drop first color; with second color, pull through last 2 lps of st.

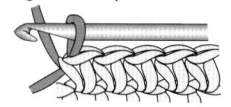

Treble crochet—tr: Yo twice, insert hook in st, yo, pull through st, [yo, pull through 2 lps] 3 times.

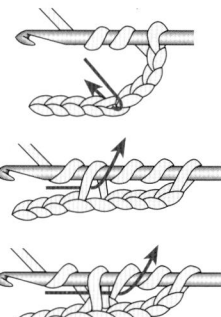
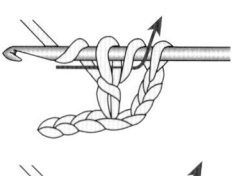
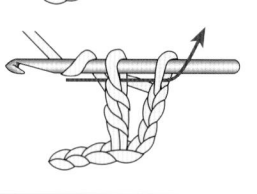

Double treble crochet—dtr: Yo 3 times, insert hook in st, yo, pull through st, [yo, pull through 2 lps] 4 times.

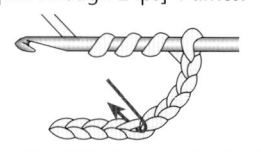

Single crochet decrease (sc dec): (Insert hook, yo, draw up a lp) in each of the sts indicated, yo, draw through all lps on hook.

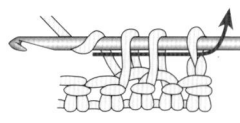
Example of 2-sc dec

Half double crochet decrease (hdc dec): (Yo, insert hook, yo, draw lp through) in each of the sts indicated, yo, draw through all lps on hook.

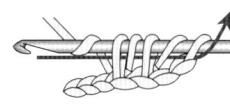
Example of 2-hdc dec

Double crochet decrease (dc dec): (Yo, insert hook, yo, draw lp through, yo, draw through 2 lps on hook) in each of the sts indicated, yo, draw through all lps on hook.

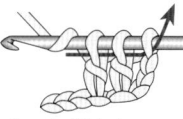
Example of 2-dc dec

US		UK
sl st (slip stitch)	=	sc (single crochet)
sc (single crochet)	=	dc (double crochet)
hdc (half double crochet)	=	htr (half treble crochet)
dc (double crochet)	=	tr (treble crochet)
tr (treble crochet)	=	dtr (double treble crochet)
dtr (double treble crochet)	=	ttr (triple treble crochet)
skip	=	miss

For more complete information, visit

StitchGuide.com